OECD ECONOMIC SURVEYS

1993-1994

PORTUGAL

ORGANISATION FOR ECONOMIC CO-OPERATION AND DEVELOPMENT

ORGANISATION FOR ECONOMIC CO-OPERATION AND DEVELOPMENT

Pursuant to Article 1 of the Convention signed in Paris on 14th December 1960, and which came into force on 30th September 1961, the Organisation for Economic Co-operation and Development (OECD) shall promote policies designed:

- to achieve the highest sustainable economic growth and employment and a rising standard of living in Member countries, while maintaining financial stability, and thus to contribute to the development of the world economy;
- to contribute to sound economic expansion in Member as well as non-member countries in the process of economic development; and
- to contribute to the expansion of world trade on a multilateral, non-discriminatory basis in accordance with international obligations.

The original Member countries of the OECD are Austria, Belgium, Canada, Denmark, France, Germany, Greece, Iceland, Ireland, Italy, Luxembourg, the Netherlands, Norway, Portugal, Spain, Sweden, Switzerland, Turkey, the United Kingdom and the United States. The following countries became Members subsequently through accession at the dates indicated hereafter: Japan (28th April 1964), Finland (28th January 1969), Australia (7th June 1971), New Zealand (29th May 1973) and Mexico (18th May 1994). The Commission of the European Communities takes part in the work of the OECD (Article 13 of the OECD Convention).

3 2280 00497 9704

Publié également en français.

Table of contents

Tables

Diagrams

Diagrams

BASIC STATISTICS OF PORTUGAL

THE LAND

Area (thousands sq. km)	92.0	Major cities, resident population in thousands (1991):	
		Greater Lisbon	1 832
		Greater Porto	1 153

THE PEOPLE

Population (1992, thousands)	9 345	Civilian employment	4 310
Number of inhabitants per sq. km	102	(1992, thousands)	
Civilian labour force (1992, thousands)	4 569	As a percentage of total:	
		Agriculture	11.4
		Industry	33.4
		Services	55.2

PRODUCTION

Gross domestic product in 1992 (million of US$)	71 450	Gross domestic product at factor cost by origin (1990, % of total):	
Gross domestic product per head in 1992 (US$):	7 646	Agriculture	5.8
Gross fixed asset formation in 1992:		Industry	37.8
% of GDP	26.0	Services	56.4
Per head (US$)	1 985		

THE GOVERNMENT

Public consumption (1992, % of GDP)	20.2	Composition of Parliament (number of seats):	
Public investment (1992, % of GDP)	4.2	Social Democrats (PSD)	135
(% of total investment)	16.2	Socialists (PS)	72
General Government current revenue		Unified Democratic Coalition (CDU)	17
1992, % of GDP	47.0	Center Social Democrats (CDS)	5
		National Solidarity (PSN)	1

FOREIGN TRADE

Exports of goods and services 1992, % of GDP	29.0	Imports of goods and services 1992, % of GDP	37.6
Main exports as a % of commodities exports, 1992 SITC:		Main imports as a % of commodities imports, 1992 SITC:	
Food, beverages and tobacco (0, 1)	7.1	Food, beverages and tobacco (0, 1)	9.8
Basic and semi-finished materials (2, 3, 4)	9.8	Basic and semi-finished materials (2, 3, 4)	12.8
Manufactured goods (5, 6, 7, 8)	82.9	Manufactured goods (5, 6, 7, 8)	75.7
of which: Chemicals (5)	4.2	of which: Chemicals (5)	9.1
Machinery and transport equipment (7)	21.6	Machinery and transport equipment (7)	37.6

THE CURRENCY

Monetary unit: Escudo		Currency units per US$ average of daily figures:	
		Year 1993	160.7
		March 1994	174.1

Note: An international comparison of certain basic statistics is given in an annex table.

This Survey is based on the Secretariat's study prepared for the annual review of Portugal by the Economic and Development Review Committee on 15th March 1994.

•

After revisions in the light of discussions during the review, final approval of the Survey for publication was given by the Committee on 31st March 1994.

•

The previous Survey of Portugal was issued in June 1993.

Introduction

Having enjoyed one of the fastest expansions in the OECD area since 1987, Portugal suffered a small fall in GDP in 1993, the first such decline since 1984. The downturn in Europe has been partly responsible, by weakening exports and business fixed investment, but domestic demand has also been depressed by high real interest rates, the squeeze on corporate profits and a deteriorating labour market. Personal consumption, which had been rather buoyant until late 1992, has been adversely affected by weaker labour demand, which pushed up unemployment to 5.5 per cent in 1993. A resumption in economic growth is dependent upon both a further global decline in interest rates and a revival of exports, but should get underway in 1994. However, as output growth is likely to remain below potential for some time, unemployment may climb further.

Weaker activity and falling nominal wage growth have helped the disinflation process, reducing the inflation gap between Portugal and the EU to 3 points by the end of 1993. However, both monetary policy and fiscal consolidation suffered setbacks in 1993 as the escudo was once again devalued and the budget deficit dramatically overshot. At nearly 8 per cent of GDP, the general government budget deficit in 1993 was nearly twice as large as projected, reversing the falling trend of public debt in terms of GDP. The economy is thus faced with an unbalanced policy mix. While exchange rate stability has remained the key intermediate target of monetary policy, and interest rates have been allowed to fall in line with European rates since mid-1993, the scope for future inflation convergence depends on the achievement of greater policy consistency, including action to enhance competition in the sheltered sectors of the economy.

This Survey begins with an examination of the factors pushing Portugal's economy into recession (Part I). Macroeconomic policies are analysed in Part II, with an emphasis both on the effects of ERM realignments and on the budgetary overshoot. The opening-up of the sheltered sector is the focus of this Survey's special chapter (Part III). While Portugal's economy has undergone substantial liberalisation since EC-membership in 1986, the strengthening of competitive pressures has been uneven across sectors, as evidenced by the persistently large differential between price increases for non-tradeables and tradeables.

I. Recent developments and prospects

Recent developments

The slowdown in economic activity, which had commenced in 1991, became more pronounced at the end of 1992. Output declined by around ¼ per cent in the second half of the year, and is estimated to have fallen further in the course of 1993. Conjunctural indicators suggest that the downswing persisted until the autumn, implying a fall in the level of GDP of around ½ per cent for the year, the first annual reduction in nearly a decade (Diagram 1). Industrial production was particularly weak, with the largest output losses recorded among producers of investment goods (Diagram 2, panel A). Capacity utilisation in manufacturing reached a six-year low of 72 per cent in mid-year, as excess stocks were run down and production prospects and orders continued to be depressed (panels B and C).

Origins of the recession

Having begun with a slowdown in the export and investment sectors, the downturn has spread to personal consumption, leading to a substantial deceleration in real domestic demand during 1993 (Table 1). Exports and investment began to lose their dynamism as early as 1991, as a consequence of a slackening external demand, increases in the real exchange rate and high real interest rates. However, domestic demand continued to expand rather rapidly until mid 1992, as household spending was sustained by increasing employment and rising real wages. Private consumption lost momentum thereafter, weakening further in the course of 1993, as evidenced by the softness in retail and car sales (Diagram 3).[1] Consumer confidence was hit by increasing uncertainty about employment prospects and declining real income gains, although the fall in consumer demand was cushioned, to some extent, by a run-down in household assets and a surge in

11

Diagram 1. **MACROECONOMIC PERFORMANCE**

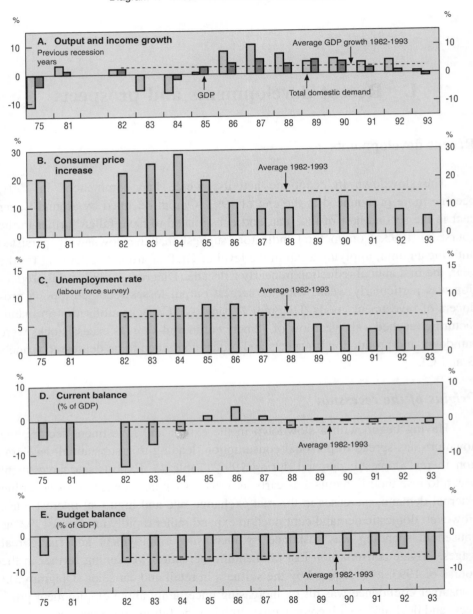

Source: OECD.

Diagram 2. **INDUSTRIAL PRODUCTION AND BUSINESS INDICATORS**

Results of business surveys

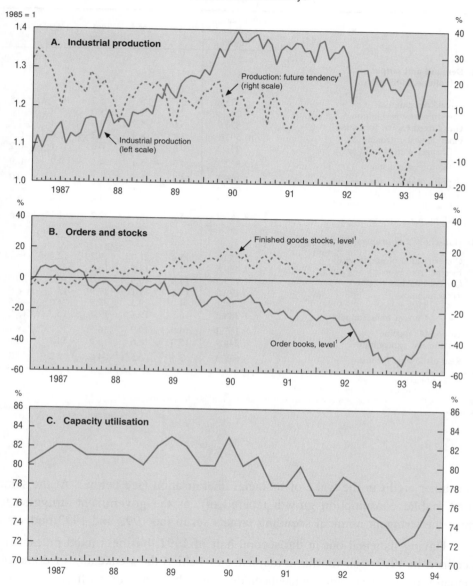

1. Per cent balance of positive and negative answers.
Source: OECD, *Main Economic Indicators.*

13

Table 1. **Recent macroeconomic developments**

Percentage changes

	1991 Current prices escudo billion	1989	1990	1991	1992	1993 [1]
A. Demand and output **(volume, 1985 prices)**						
Private consumption	6 273.8	3.3	5.3	5.2	3.7	0.5
Government consumption	1 742.4	2.8	1.5	3.0	1.4	0.4
Gross fixed capital formation	2 574.9	5.6	5.9	2.5	5.4	–4.7
Final domestic demand	10 591.1	3.8	4.9	4.3	3.8	–0.8
Change in stockbuilding [2]	231.2	0.6	0.7	0.0	1.1	–0.2
Total domestic demand	10 822.3	4.3	5.4	4.1	4.7	–0.9
Exports of goods and services	3 166.3	13.3	9.5	1.1	6.1	0.0
Imports of goods and services	4 098.7	9.1	10.1	4.9	11.1	–0.9
Change in foreign balance [2]	–932.4	0.2	–1.9	–2.6	–4.5	0.7
GDP at market prices	9 889.9	5.2	4.4	2.2	1.1	–0.5
B. Household's appropriation account						
Compensation of employees	4 550.5	15.4	21.0	19.2	12.4	5.7
Income from property and others	3 429.8	22.3	18.1	16.0	13.5	3.0
Current transfers received	2 219.2	14.8	16.8	18.0	16.5	20.0
Total income	10 199.5	17.5	19.1	17.9	13.7	8.0
less: Direct taxes	704.1	44.7	9.2	37.5	24.8	–4.5
Current transfers paid	1 388.2	16.3	19.1	17.7	16.7	13.8
Disposable income	8 167.3	16.0	19.9	16.5	12.2	8.1
Consumers' expenditure	6 244.9	15.8	18.6	16.9	14.7	8.0
Real disposable income	3 637.3	3.5	6.5	4.8	2.2	1.3

1. OECD estimates.
2. As a per cent of GDP in the previous period.
Source: OECD, *National Accounts* and estimates; and National Institute of Statistics.

consumer credit in the wake of financial liberalisation (see below). At the same time, public consumption growth tapered off, as the government struggled to meet the stringent nominal spending targets set in the 1992 and 1993 budgets.

Having flattened out in the second half of 1992, business fixed investment declined in 1993, constituting a major factor behind the weakening of domestic demand. Business confidence has been depressed by shrinking profit margins and persistently high costs of borrowing, as well as deteriorating prospects for internal and external demand. Indicators of investment activity point both to a drop in

Diagram 3. **CONJUNCTURAL INDICATORS OF DEMAND**

Year-on-year growth rate, per cent

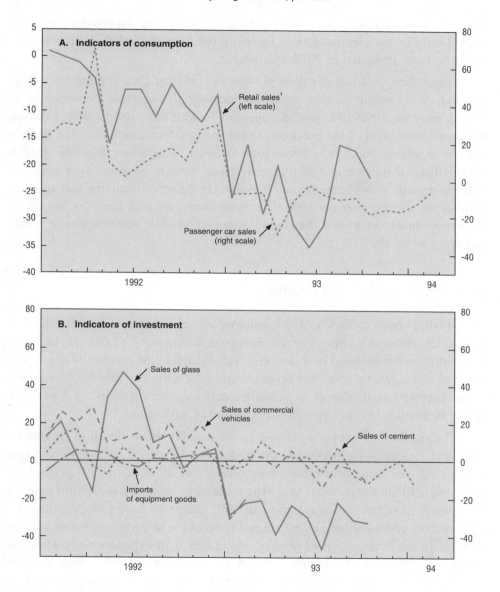

1. Balance of positive and negative opinions.
Source: Bank of Portugal, *Monthly Bulletin.*

15

equipment investment and continued weakness of construction investment (Diagram 3). In April 1993, the Government announced measures to stimulate investment in public housing and infrastructure, but these are expected to have an impact only in the medium term. Overall, gross fixed capital formation is estimated to have stagnated in 1993 as a whole.

Given the slowdown in export growth, but buoyant consumption-led import demand, the foreign balance made an increasingly negative contribution to growth over the 1990-1992 period (Diagram 1). Due to statistical delays caused by the establishment of the European single market, firm data on foreign trade is not yet available for 1993. There are, however, indications that the growth contribution of the foreign balance may have become positive, as a result of reduced growth in consumption and imports. On the other hand, the real appreciation of the escudo over the 1990-92 period, combined with the slow growth of the European export market, has led to a stagnation of export volumes of goods and services in 1993.

The labour market and inflation

Having begun to slow in 1992, employment contracted in 1993 for the first time since Portugal's entry into the European Community (Table 2). In 1993, total employment declined by 2 per cent, with the fall in the number of dependent workers outweighing small employment gains among the self-employed. Job losses occurred in all sectors of economic activity, ranging from a 2.7 per cent fall in industry to 1.6 per cent in services and in agriculture.

The number of unemployed has grown steadily since the third quarter of 1992 and, despite some decline in the participation rate, the unemployment rate reached 5.5 per cent for the first three quarters of 1993, about 1.5 percentage points higher than the previous year. The reversal of the previous upward trend in the participation rate which occurred in 1992 seems to have reflected discouraged-worker effects among men, increasing recourse to early retirement and an increase in the average school-leaving age in line with experience elsewhere in Europe. The number of first-time job seekers decreased in 1993, so that the rise in unemployment has mainly reflected the greater numbers of workers seeking to replace lost jobs. Moreover, the severity of the downturn in labour demand can be seen in the increasing number of laid-off workers (as opposed to those whose

Table 2. **Labour-market indicators**

Percentages

	1988	1989	1990	1991	1992 [1]	1993
Labour force (growth rate)	1.1	1.5	1.8	2.4	..	-0.5
Male	0.2	1.4	0.9	0.7	..	-1.4
Female	2.5	1.6	2.9	4.0	..	-6.0
Employment (growth rate)	2.6	2.2	2.3	3.0	0.9 [2]	-2.0
Male	1.5	2.0	1.4	1.4	0.3 [2]	-2.6
Female	4.1	2.5	3.5	5.1	1.8 [2]	-1.1
Dependent employment (growth rate)	4.4	3.5	2.9	1.4	0.8 [2]	-2.8
Agriculture	-4.4	-6.3	-4.1	0.6	-2.3 [2]	-1.6
Industry	3.3	2.9	0.9	0.4	-0.2 [2]	-2.8
Services	5.5	5.8	5.9	6.0	2.3 [2]	-1.7
Unemployment rate [3]	5.7	5.0	4.6	4.1	4.1	5.5
Male	4.0	3.3	3.1	2.7	3.4	4.7
Female	8.0	7.2	6.6	5.8	4.9	6.5
Youth	11.5	11.4	10.0	9.1	10.0	12.7
Long-term (+12 months) [4]	44.7	40.9	31.5	30.7	26.8	29.3
Participation rate [5]	69.0	69.5	70.1	71.6	68.4	67.8
Male	81.2	81.9	82.0	82.2	78.7	77.4
Female	57.5	58.0	59.0	61.6	58.9	58.9
Job vacancies [6]	0.21	0.21	0.16	0.17	0.15	0.15

1. Break in series.
2. Estimates by INE.
3. Per cent of working-age population.
4. Per cent of total registered unemployment.
5. Defined as 15 to 64 years old up to 1991 and as 16 to 64 year old afterwards.
6. As a percentage of the labour force.
Source: OECD, *Labour Force Statistics*; OECD, *Employment Outlook*; and Portuguese authorities.

fixed-term contract expired), as well as in the decreasing number of job vacancies.

Although rising, the Portuguese unemployment rate remains significantly below the OECD average. This relatively good performance has been largely a result of a flexible labour market:

- Real wage growth is more sensitive to changes in unemployment than elsewhere in Europe,[2] partly reflecting the close link between wage settlements and productivity growth. Wage differentials across sectors have increased over the last decade and are wider than in other European countries.[3]

- National labour agreements may have damped wage inflation in years of severe labour-market pressure.
- Possible disincentives to job search are limited, unemployment compensation being low in absolute terms and in relation to the level of minimum wages.[4]

The favourable labour market outcome in the 1980s was achieved, even though Portugal had the most restrictive job protection legislation in the European Community. In 1989 firing restrictions were eased through a wider range of admissible lay-off motivations, the possibility of collective lay-offs and easier resolution of severance pay disagreements.

Nominal wage growth decelerated sharply in 1993, reflecting the easing of labour market conditions. Pay rises implicit in collective wage settlements for the economy as a whole slowed to 7 per cent, the pace of disinflation in private sector contractual wages being most marked in some services, and construction, activities where nominal wage growth had previously been more pronounced (Table 3). Moreover, workers not covered by collective agreements are likely to have received lower pay increases. Together with a pick up in productivity, nominal wage deceleration further curbed the rise in unit labour costs in the business sector to an estimated 7.2 per cent in 1993. For the total economy, the rise in unit labour costs was much larger, reflecting an exceptional hike in non-wage labour costs due to higher pension contributions in the public sector. This more than offset the impact of more effective wage containment in the government sector, where the effects of the 1989 pay reform began to tail off and the rise in wages diminished sharply.

Consumer-price inflation (excluding rent) was still around 9 per cent in 1992, but with domestic cost pressures subsiding, it abated rapidly in the first six months of 1993, bottoming out at 5.6 per cent in June, the lowest rate in more than two decades. In the second half of the year, disinflation came to a halt, as currency depreciation reversed the fall in import prices (Diagram 4). The 12-month inflation rate in December, at 6.5 per cent, was nonetheless still below the 7 per cent upper bound of the target range. The Government thus met its inflation objective for the second consecutive year, reducing the inflation differ-

Table 3. **Wage and price developments**

Per cent rate of growth

	1988	1989	1990	1991	1992	1993 [1]
Total compensation	14.6	15.4	21.0	19.2	12.4	5.7
Private compensation per employee	7.2	10.4	17.3	15.4	13.7	7.3
Contractual wages	9.1	10.5	13.7	14.2	11.3	7.3
Unit labour costs (business sector)	7.7	8.0	15.3	14.1	10.1	7.2
Unit labour costs (manufacturing)	9.8	9.0	13.0	13.0	10.0	7.0
Private consumption deflator	10.0	12.1	12.6	11.1	9.8	6.7
Projected inflation [2]	6.0	6.0	10.0	10.8	9.3	6.5
Import prices	11.6	8.6	6.5	1.2	−3.4	4.0
Export prices	8.9	10.8	6.1	1.0	−1.7	2.9
GDP deflator	11.6	13.0	14.3	14.1	14.0	6.5
Memorandum item:						
Labour productivity (total economy) [3]	1.3	2.9	2.2	−0.9	0.6	0.7
Labour productivity (manufacturing) [3]	−0.2	−0.5	4.2	−2.0	−3.0	..

1. OECD estimates.
2. Budget projections for consumer prices excluding rent.
3. Break in employment series in 1992.
Source: OECD, *National Accounts*; and Ministry of Finance.

ential with the rest of the EC to just above 3 points from 4.4 points in 1992. Nevertheless, strong inflationary pressures still emanated from the service sector, where in December 1993 the 12-month rise in prices was around 10 per cent.

Reflecting the improvement in the terms of trade during the initial stages of the economic slowdown, real wage gains in the private sector remained significant in 1991 and 1992, but eased gradually with the rise in unemployment and almost came to a standstill in 1993 (Diagram 5). However, the process of real wage adjustment may not be sufficiently rapid to ensure a quick reabsorption of unemployment.

Foreign trade and the current balance

After the adoption of the floating exchange rate regime in October 1990, losses in competitiveness contributed to a slowing in the rapid pace of gains in Portuguese export market shares experienced in the late 1980s (Table 4). Between 1990, when the crawling-peg policy was abandoned, and the end of 1992, the real effective exchange rate appreciated by around 21 per cent, as

Diagram 4. **INFLATION DEVELOPMENTS**

Year-on-year percentage changes

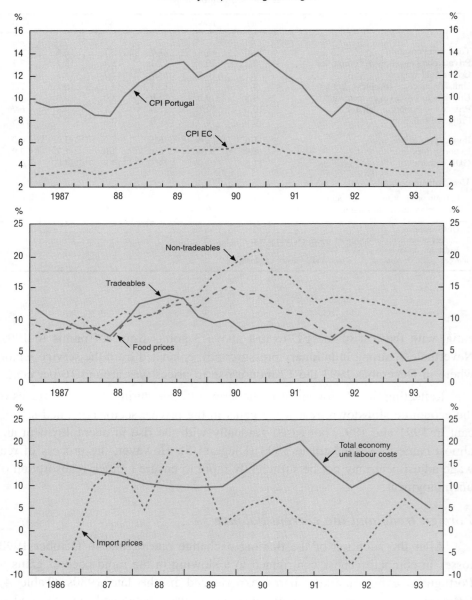

Source: Bank of Portugal and OECD.

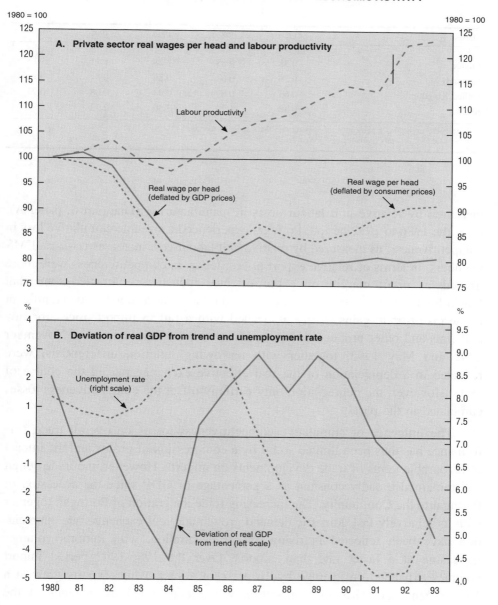

Diagram 5. **REAL WAGES, PRODUCTIVITY AND ECONOMIC ACTIVITY**

1980 = 100

125

A. Private sector real wages per head and labour productivity

120

115

110

105

100

95

90

Labour productivity[1]

Real wage per head
(deflated by GDP prices)

Real wage per head
(deflated by consumer prices)

85

80

75

%

4

B. Deviation of real GDP from trend and unemployment rate

3

2

Unemployment rate
(right scale)

1

0

-1

-2

-3

Deviation of real GDP
from trend (left scale)

-4

-5

1980   81   82   83   84   85   86   87   88   89   90   91   92   93

1. Break in the Labour Force series in 1992.
Source: OECD.

21

Table 4. **Export market shares**[1]

Per cent

Market	1980	1986	1990	1991	1992
France	0.38	0.88	1.28	1.11	1.13
Germany	0.36	0.64	0.86	0.87	0.93
United Kingdom	0.65	0.89	0.93	0.88	0.93
Spain	0.48	1.29	2.50	2.72	2.71

1. Portuguese exports as a percentage of imports into the respective market.
Source: OECD, Monthly Statistics of Foreign Trade.

measured by relative unit labour costs in manufacturing (Diagram 6, panel A). Over the 1986 to 1992 period, Portugal experienced a sizeable cumulative loss in competitiveness, as measured by relative unit labour cost increases vis-à-vis EMS members. In terms of relative export prices, losses in competitiveness were more limited, as profit margins in export-oriented industries contracted somewhat (panel B). Cost pressures were reduced by the fact that Portugal made significant net terms-of-trade gains, partly associated with a fall in import prices for raw materials and other production inputs. Moreover, the devaluations of November 1992 and May 1993, together with narrowing inflation differentials, were reflected in a depreciation of the real effective exchange rate in the course of 1993. However, the depreciation only partially offset the competitiveness losses cumulated in the past.

The influence of cumulative competitiveness losses on overall trade performance has thus been limited so far by a compression of profits and the impact of favourable terms of trade developments on imports. However, the trade deficit had remained broadly constant as a percentage of GDP since the accession of Portugal to the Community. The increasing trade integration of Portugal, together with its relatively fast domestic demand growth and real-exchange rate appreciation have been reflected in rising import penetration, with imports volumes increasing at a faster rate than exports. Over the 1986-1992 period import volumes expanded on average by 16 per cent a year, while exports grew at a 10 per cent rate. Growing integration was accompanied by changes in the regional distribution of Portuguese trade, with an increasing share taken by Portugal's EC partners (Table 5). Modifications have also occurred in the compo-

Diagram 6. **INDICATORS OF COMPETITIVENESS AND FOREIGN TRADE**

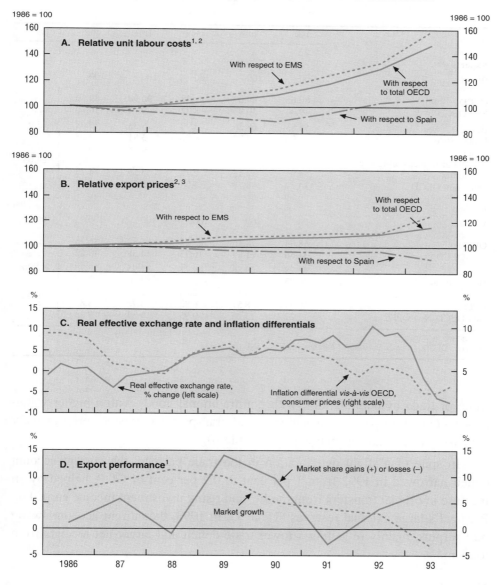

1986 = 100

A. Relative unit labour costs[1,2]

With respect to EMS

With respect to total OECD

With respect to Spain

1986 = 100

B. Relative export prices[2,3]

With respect to total OECD

With respect to EMS

With respect to Spain

%

C. Real effective exchange rate and inflation differentials

Real effective exchange rate, % change (left scale)

Inflation differential *vis-à-vis* OECD, consumer prices (right scale)

%

D. Export performance[1]

Market share gains (+) or losses (−)

Market growth

1986   87   88   89   90   91   92   93

1. Manufacturing.
2. In a common currency.
3. Goods and services.
Source: OECD estimates.

23

Table 5. **Trade by regions**

As a percentage of total trade

	1980	1986	1990	1991	1992	1993[1]
Exports						
World	100	100	100	100	100	100
OECD	80.66	89.07	91.28	90.90	89.30	..
Non-OECD	19.34	10.93	8.72	9.10	10.70	..
EC-12	58.85	68.26	73.99	75.33	75.08	75.97
United States	5.70	7.02	4.82	3.81	3.48	
Japan	0.92	0.83	1.03	0.88	0.77	
Brazil and former Portuguese colonies	4.97	2.15	2.77	3.59	4.73	24.03
Other non-OECD	14.37	8.78	5.95	5.51	5.97	
Imports						
World	100	100	100	100	100	100
OECD	68.34	78.15	83.23	85.42	86.78	..
Non-OECD	31.66	21.85	16.77	14.58	13.22	..
EC-12	45.28	58.86	69.21	71.95	73.75	72.00
United States	10.93	6.84	3.92	3.40	3.02	
Japan	3.05	3.57	2.64	2.90	3.06	
OPEC	19.44	8.57	6.82	4.75	3.87	28.00
Non-OECD Non-OPEC	12.22	13.28	9.95	9.83	9.35	

1. First ten months.
Source: OECD, *Monthly Statistics of Foreign Trade* and INE (for 1993).

sition of trade by commodities, with non-traditional goods with a higher value-added content (especially machinery and transport equipment) progressively increasing as a share of total exports (Table 6).

In spite of a slight deterioration in the trade balance, the current account deficit narrowed in 1992 from 1 per cent to 0.2 per cent of GDP, helped by an increase in official transfers from the EC and rising investment income earned on Portugal's large external reserves (Table 7). In 1993, the current account swang into surplus, mainly reflecting a lower trade deficit and larger net receipts from tourism.[5]

Capital movements

Following large capital inflows in 1990 and 1991, associated with relatively high Portuguese interest rates, the balance on medium- and long-term capital

Table 6. **Trade by commodities**

As a percentage of total value trade

	1989	1990	1991	1992
Exports				
Food, live animals, beverages and tobacco	7.10	6.65	7.24	7.09
Crude materials, inedible, animal and vegetable oils and fats	10.80	9.42	7.87	7.20
Mineral fuels, lubricants and related materials	3.36	3.47	2.61	2.82
Chemicals, manufactured goods excluding machinery and transport equipment	60.22	61.11	62.74	61.28
Machinery and transport equipment	18.51	19.34	19.53	21.60
Imports				
Food, live animals, beverages and tobacco	9.90	9.67	11.14	11.08
Crude materials, inedible, animal and vegetable oils and fats	7.04	6.10	5.53	4.58
Mineral fuels, lubricants and related materials	10.45	11.01	8.82	8.19
Chemicals, manufactured goods excluding machinery and transport equipment	35.95	36.93	38.08	38.16
Machinery and transport equipment	36.65	36.30	36.42	37.98

Source: OECD, *Foreign Trade by Commodities.*

Table 7. **Balance of payments**

Billion escudos

	1990	1991	1992	1993
Exports (fob)	2 320	2 339	2 450	2 479
Imports (fob)	3 287	3 473	3 732	3 574
Trade balance	−968	−1 134	−1 281	−1 095
Services, net	160	171	209	192
of which: Tourism	380	391	341	378
Investment income, net	−34	11	90	−7
Transfers, net	782	868	1 059	1 078
Private	638	666	643	619
Public	144	202	414	459
Current balance	−26	−96	−23	168
(as a per cent of GDP)	(−0.3)	(−1.0)	(−0.2)	(1.4)
Medium- and long-term capital, net	511	587	−45	139
of which: Foreign direct investment, net	321	331	262	222
Basic balance	485	492	−68	307
Short-term capital and unrecorded transactions, net	80	263	140	94
Balance on non-monetary transactions	565	754	72	401
Short-term capital of private monetary institutions, net	−47	113	−71	−619
Balance on official settlements	518	868	1	−218

Source: Bank of Portugal.

25

moved into deficit in 1992, as non-residents sold domestic securities in anticipation of a currency depreciation and net foreign direct investment declined from the high levels experienced in the past. Direct investment, especially in finance and real estate, continued to decline in 1993, partly reflecting cyclical factors, the slowdown in privatisations and the end of capital controls, which in the past had been partly circumvented by investors using the direct investment channel. Indeed, in spite of the decline in direct foreign investment and the renewed pressures prior to the second realignment of the escudo in May, substantial demand for domestic securities by non-residents shifted the basic balance into surplus in 1993, after turning into deficit to the tune of 0.5 per cent of GDP in 1992.

The balance on short-term capital plunged into deficit in 1993, pulled down by an increase in bank credit to non-residents in escudos (especially to foreign branches of Portuguese banks), largely reflecting hedging behaviour by financial institutions and the opening of deposit accounts abroad by non-financial residents in the wake of financial liberalisation. In this way, Portuguese banks may partly have circumvented the limits set by the central bank on net foreign exchange currency positions of domestic banks. Thus, on a consolidated basis, banks increased their long foreign exchange positions by a substantial amount. Partly as a result, having returned to balance in 1992 after several years of sizeable surpluses, the overall balance of payments was in deficit in 1993.

The outlook to 1995

OECD projections are based on the assumption that budget deficit targets will be broadly met in 1994 and 1995, with the Government adopting corrective measures if necessary in the event of unfavourable developments (Table 8). Assisted by a shift to fiscal restraint and growing labour market slack, the stance of monetary policy is expected to become less restrictive, with nominal interest rates projected to fall in line with German rates and the risk premia attaching to domestic interest rates assumed to ease somewhat.

Against this background, output growth may gradually recover from the trough in 1993, firming in 1994 and 1995, though remaining well below potential. The main demand forces seen as shaping the revival of output growth include a stronger performance of exports and private consumption, in turn

Table 8. Short-term projections

Percentage changes

	1992	1993	1994	1995
Demand and output				
Private consumption	3.7	0.5	1.8	2.7
Public consumption	1.4	0.4	1.0	1.1
Gross fixed investment	5.4	-4.7	3.5	4.8
Final domestic demand	3.8	-0.8	2.1	3.0
Stockbuilding[1]	1.1	-0.2	0.0	0.1
Total domestic demand	4.7	-0.9	2.0	3.0
Exports of goods and services	6.1	0.0	4.5	8.5
Imports of goods and services	11.1	-0.9	4.8	7.6
Foreign balance[1]	-4.5	0.7	-1.3	-1.4
GDP at market prices	1.1	-0.5	1.2	2.3
Industrial production	-3.0	-4.0	1.7	3.1
Prices				
GDP price deflator	13.5	6.4	5.6	4.6
Private consumption deflator	9.8	6.7	5.7	4.4
Unemployment rate	4.2	5.5	6.4	6.9
	Billions of escudos			
General government financial balance	-530.6	-941.8	-963.1	-908.6
As a percentage of GDP[2]	-4.7	-7.8	-7.5	-6.6

1. As a percentage of GDP in the previous period.
2. Based upon old national accounts data.
Source: OECD projections.

stimulating gross fixed investment. Falling interest rates should support private consumption growth in 1994, with a resumption in employment gains strengthening the expansion of consumer spending in 1995. With a stronger expansion of export markets, and helped by a growing surplus of the invisible balance, the current account surplus may widen in 1994. While the last semi-annual survey of October 1993 portrayed a rather pessimistic picture of private investment intentions, EU-financed investment and public capital expenditure may more than offset protracted investment weakness in the private sector.

With output continuing to grow below potential, the unemployment rate may climb further to around 7 per cent in 1995. Given the substantial slack in goods markets and the traditionally strong response of nominal wage growth to unemployment, the rise in consumer prices is projected to fall to between 5½ and 6 per cent in 1994, as the effects from currency depreciation finish working through, declining to under 5 per cent in 1995. Real wages are likely to grow more slowly than labour productivity, alleviating pressures on profit margins.

The major risk attaching to the projections concerns fiscal policy. Any failure to resume fiscal consolidation after the severe setback in 1993 would endanger the convergence of inflation and interest rates to European levels. An interruption to the declining trend of interest rates would negatively affect the pick up in economic activity. The background to these risks is more fully discussed in the next section.

II. Macroeconomic policies

Overview

1993 was characterised by setbacks to monetary and fiscal policy. Fiscal consolidation suffered a severe reverse, as falling output and tax evasion contributed to a deficit overrun of $3\frac{1}{2}$ per cent of GDP. The fiscal slippage would, in itself, have narrowed the scope for steering interest rates down to levels more commensurate with the cyclical weakness of the economy. Additionally, however, in the spring of 1993, renewed turbulence on European exchange markets led to further downward pressure on the escudo and prompted a temporary tightening of monetary conditions. The escudo was devalued relative to the strongest EMS currencies in May, the second parity adjustment in six months (Diagram 7). Subsequently, the authorities have reasserted the commitment to exchange rate stability as a key intermediate target of monetary policy. Following the widening of the ERM band in August 1993, the escudo continued to trade within the old intervention limits. Short-term interest rate differentials have been slow to narrow.

Portuguese interest rates currently need to be at substantial premium over EC rates in order to maintain the existing parity. Moreover, higher-than-average rates of inflation and budget deficit severely limit the scope for cutting official lending rates ahead of European rates without exposing the escudo to renewed downward pressure within the new ERM bands. While real wage flexibility will reduce the cost of adhering to the exchange rate target, the two devaluations mean that prospects for a further rapid reduction in inflation expectations have deteriorated. In these circumstances, the most effective way to reduce interest rates would seem to be through a better-balanced policy mix, based on a tighter fiscal stance. Prospects for the budget are appraised in the second half of this chapter, following a discussion of monetary and exchange-rate developments.

Diagram 7. **EXCHANGE-RATE AND INTEREST-RATE DEVELOPMENTS**

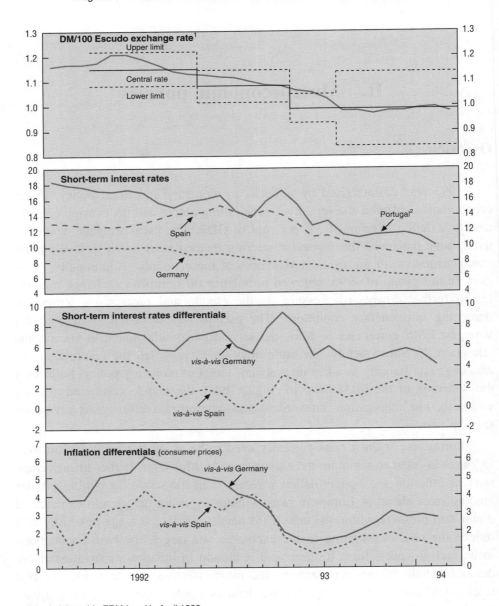

1. Escudo joins wide ERM-band in April 1992.
2. 3-month Interbank money market rate (86 to 96 days).
Source: OECD.

Monetary and exchange-rate policy

With the escudo participating in the Exchange Rate Mechanism since April 1992 and all restrictions on capital movements removed, domestic monetary conditions have been essentially subordinated to external developments: in principle, exchange-rate targeting means that the central bank has to respond to movements in official reserves rather than domestic liquidity conditions. Occasionally, however, the Portuguese monetary authorities have been under strong pressure to use their available room for manœuvre to ease the monetary stance in line with cyclical conditions. The Bank has at times found it difficult to reconcile the objective of exchange rate stability with lower interest rates. Indeed, in early 1993 interest rates on money market instruments were not immediately utilised to the extent necessary to counter heavy exchange rate pressure on the escudo and a gradual depreciation was allowed to take place even before the ERM realignment.[6] By contrast, following the adoption of wider ERM bands, market expectations of a steep decline in interest rates and further currency depreciation were not fulfilled.

Interest rate developments and open-market operations

Financial deregulation and exchange-rate targeting have altered the operational basis of monetary policies. Beginning in 1989, the authorities have gradually dismantled direct monetary controls, replacing them with a system of indirect control, via open market operations. Since the abolition of credit ceilings and credit growth recommendations in 1990, policy has focused on the setting of cash reserves for the banking system in order to influence the growth of liquidity,[7] the transition to indirect monetary control being accomplished in 1992 with the removal of remaining capital controls and interest rate regulations.[8] At the same time, policy has needed to be implemented with greater flexibility, both because financial liberalisation has reduced the information content of monetary aggregates and because the combination of capital market liberalisation and exchange rate targeting has caused substantial instability in the level of foreign exchange reserves. New instruments had to be developed to control domestic liquidity, which ballooned in 1991 because of substantial capital inflows. In 1991 and the first half of 1992, the Bank of Portugal used Treasury bills for purposes of absorbing liquidity. Since joining the ERM and liberalising capital movements, the authorities have ceased to specify targets for liquidity growth.

Following the currency turmoil and devaluation in late 1992, developments in early 1993 pointed to renewed confidence in the escudo, and the Bank of Portugal intervened to sell escudos as official reserves rose. This allowed the Bank to go ahead with a gradual and systematic reduction in money market intervention rates. However, sentiment changed from mid-February onwards, as downward pressure on the escudo returned. This pressure was initially met principally by intervention, the Bank being under pressure not to take action that would further weaken the economy. The interest rate response was limited to a slight increase in official rates. This proved insufficient, however. The rate on occasional operations was pushed up to over 20 per cent by April, but this was not enough to prevent a gradual slide in the effective rate of the escudo within the intervention limits.

Devaluation followed in May, and the stabilisation of the foreign exchange market thereafter allowed official interest rates to be cut sharply and immediately. By February 1994, the regular liquidity absorption rate had been reduced in several steps to 9 per cent, 5 points below the rate applied before the first devaluation of the escudo in November 1992 (Table 9). Over the same period, the Bank has also adjusted the rates for liquidity injection. In the first half of the year, the Bank was active in providing occasional injections of liquidity to compensate, in part, for the destruction of the monetary base caused by repeated foreign exchange intervention to support the escudo. Suspended by the end of July due to exchange market turmoil, regular liquidity injections were resumed in late October at a rate of 11.25 per cent, falling to 10.25 per cent in February 1994. Since August 1992, the rate for regular liquidity injection has been lowered by nearly 6 points, as volatility subsided and liquidity conditions became more normal, further reducing the spread between the absorption and injection rates.

In July 1993, the Bank of Portugal again suspended its regular interventions in the money market, introducing a new facility, called the automatic provision of liquidity or "daily facility", to complement central bank certificates used for purposes of controlling liquidity. Designed to smooth interest rates over the reserve requirement period, the facility puts an effective upper limit on money market rates.[9] In February 1994, the rate on the new "daily facility" stood at 11.5 per cent, down from 14.5 per cent in July.[10] The Bank of Portugal has also

Table 9. **Money-market intervention and lending rates**[1]

	Regular liquidity absorption rate (intervention rate)	Rate for regular provision of liquidity (lending rate)	Rate of remuneration of minimum cash reserves
1991			
September	16.000	20.750	
October	15.750	20.250	15.750
November	15.625	20.000	
1992			
February		19.500	
March		18.938	
April	15.375	17.938	15.375
July	15.250	17.750	14.500
August	15.000	17.000	
	14.000	16.000	
September	suspended	suspended	
October	14.000		13.250
November	suspended		
December	14.000		
1993			
January	13.625		12.875
	13.250		
	13.000		
February	12.750		
	13.000		
March	13.500		
	suspended		
May	17.000		
	13.000		
	12.000		
June	11.250		
	11.000		
	10.500		
July	10.250	11.250	9.875
	suspended	suspended	
October	10.375	11.250	
November	10.250	11.250	
December	10.000	11.000	
1994			
January	9.875	10.875	
	9.750	10.750	
	9.500	10.500	
February	9.250	10.250	

1. Introduced in April 1991.
Source: Bank of Portugal (1993), *Monthly Bulletin*, various issues, Table 4.12.

reduced the rate of remuneration on cash reserves, in two steps, by 3.375 points. Under the modification of the reserve system announced in April 1994, compulsory reserves will be cut sharply from the current level of 17 per cent, thereby reducing a comparative disadvantage of Portuguese banks *vis-à-vis* EC competitors.[11]

The reduction in official interest rates since October 1992 has been fully mirrored in the fall in the three-month interbank rate, which eased to 11.7 per cent in December 1993, 5.6 points above the German equivalent (Diagram 8). The short-term interest differential *vis-à-vis* Germany changed little in the second half of 1993, but narrowed in early 1994. In the primary market, interest rates for 7- and 10-year Treasury bonds eased, helped by expectations of the elimination of the 20 per cent withholding tax on government paper for non-residents. Rates applied to best customers (CRISTAL loans) also dropped sharply but the decline has been less pronounced for some corporate interest rates, including the APB-indicative lending rate[12] and the rate on the discount of commercial bills.

The relatively modest decline in lending rates stemmed from the augmented default risk of some companies, manifest in a rise in non-performing loans. Overall, nominal rates have fallen in line with consumer-price inflation – real lending rates remained broadly unchanged in 1993 –, while real deposit rates have declined, perhaps contributing to the fall in the household savings ratio.

Evolution of money and credit

The rapid growth of credit to firms and individuals continued unabated in the first half of 1993, ebbing thereafter to 13.3 per cent in December compared with 19 per cent in the same month of 1992 (Diagram 9). Underlying this continued strength were both structural and cyclical factors, including the removal of restrictions on consumer credit and a shift of credit to sectors less hit by the recession. Credits to the service-producing sector soared by about 30 per cent in the first nine months of 1993 compared with a year earlier. In contrast, the rise in credits to industry fell to 2 per cent in this period.

Together with a negative contribution from the external side, resulting from capital outflows and the deficit on current account, the slower pace of credit expansion was responsible for damping the rise in domestic liquidity: in December 1993, growth in L- (liquid assets held by non-financial residents) was 8 per cent, down from 12.8 per cent in December 1992. The expansion of M1 also

Diagram 8. **INTEREST RATES**

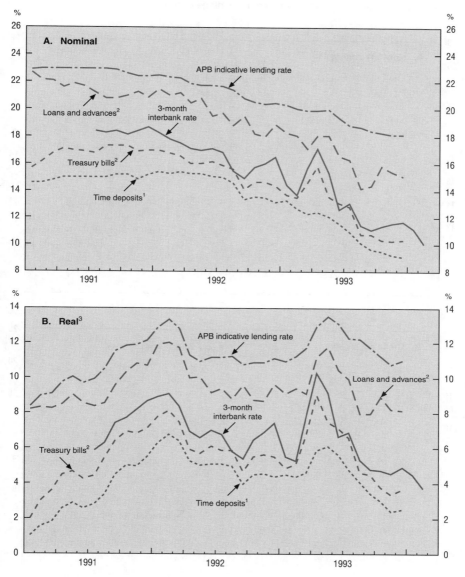

1. 181 days up to one year.
2. 91 days up to 180 days.
3. Adjusted for year-on-year change of the consumer price index.
Source: Bank of Portugal and OECD.

35

Diagram 9. MONETARY AND CREDIT AGGREGATES

Year-on-year percentage changes

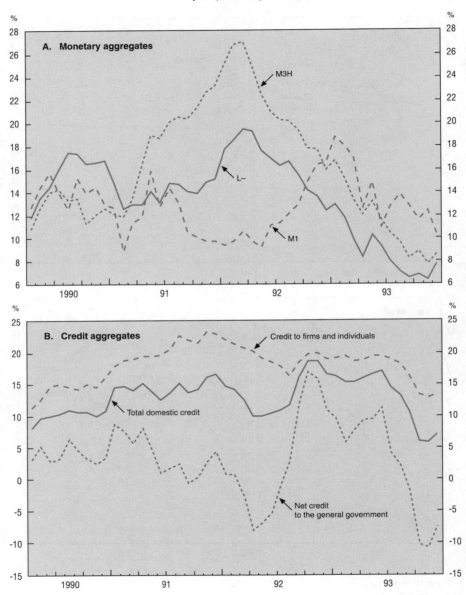

Source: Bank of Portugal.

slackened in 1993 especially in the first half, in contrast to the previous year when a relative rise in demand deposit rates, stemming from the liberalisation of interest rates on such deposits in May 1992, had fuelled the growth of M1 at a time when overall liquidity growth was already subsiding.[13]

Exchange-rate developments

The easing in monetary conditions during 1993 was accompanied by a significant depreciation in the Portuguese currency (Diagram 10). The nominal effective exchange rate, based upon trade shares with 27 countries, slipped by 2.4 per cent in the first half of 1993 from the previous six months, the first half-yearly decline since 1990, when Portugal abandoned its thirteen-year old regime of small, pre-announced currency depreciations. The renewed decline in the effective exchange rate owed much to the second devaluation in May 1993, which reduced the central value of the escudo in the ERM by 6.5 per cent, somewhat less than the simultaneous devaluation of the Spanish peseta (8 per cent), but slightly above the previous parity adjustment in November 1992 (6 per cent).[14]

The fall in the nominal effective exchange rate steepened as the ERM fluctuation bands widened in August 1993, reaching 7 per cent in the second half of 1993. For the year as a whole, currency depreciation totalled 5.5 per cent, implying a fall in the real exchange rate of 2.6 per cent, the first decline since 1981 (see Part I). Since September, the currency has remained reasonably stable, reflecting the relatively tight stance of monetary policy. Market sentiment, though, has remained volatile, as evidenced by the sudden attack on the escudo in early April 1994.

Fiscal policy

In line with the medium-term convergence programme drawn up in 1991 (QUANTUM2), the Government had planned in the 1993 budget to lower the general government deficit ratio to 4.3 per cent of GDP in 1993, by meeting stringent nominal primary spending targets while collecting revenues at a rate only slightly below income growth.[15] Official estimates suggest, however, that after several years in which budgetary outcomes were in line with targets, the

Diagram 10. **ESCUDO EXCHANGE RATES**

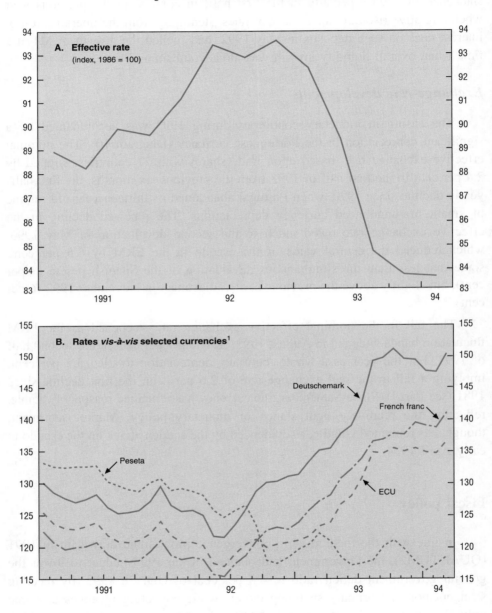

1. Escudos per unit of foreign currency, 1986 = 100.
Source: OECD estimates.

Diagram 11. **TARGETS AND OUTTURNS**[1]

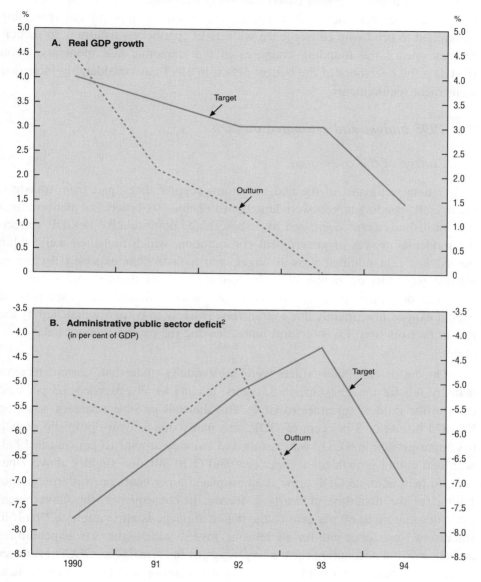

1. The targets for each calendar year are as presented in the Finance Ministry's *Orcamento do Estado* for that year which is published in October of the previous year.
2. Public accounts basis. Global balance excluding financial transactions.
Source: Ministerio das Finanças.

deficit (on a public accounts basis) massively overshot, reaching Esc 1 017 billion or 8.5 per cent of GDP (Diagram 11). With the government remaining committed to achieving convergence with its EC partners – its aim is to participate as one of the founding countries in the economic and monetary union (EMU) – the overshoot of the budget deficit in 1993 has considerably increased adjustment requirements.

The 1993 budget and estimated outturn

Causes of the overshoot

Official estimates of the budget outturn suggest that, apart from transfers, the overall spending targets were largely met (Table 10). Indeed, as planned, total current disbursements decreased by ½ percentage point relative to GDP, reflecting moderate growth of government consumption, which remained well within the 10 per cent nominal growth target, and a faster-than-expected decline in interest payments on public debt. In contrast, current transfers surged as the recession deepened, pushing up the social security deficit. The overshoot in capital expenditure, mainly due to transfers, is likely to be partly matched by the rise in receipts from EC structural funds, leaving the capital account balance on target.

On the revenue side targets were substantially undershot: current receipts actually fell for the first time in 35 years, leading to an estimated 3.3 per cent drop in the ratio of revenues to GDP. The shortfall in State revenues, totalling Esc 374 billion or 3 per cent of GDP, was partly due to over-optimistic growth assumptions: nominal GDP was assumed to grow by around 10 per cent in 1993, with real output growth set at 3 per cent and GDP inflation slightly above 7 per cent. In fact, nominal GDP grew at an estimated 5 per cent rate, with real output falling for the first time in nearly a decade. In consequence, the Government estimates that up to 60 per cent of the deficit slippage is attributable to "built-in stabilisers" and once-and-for-all revenue losses, with higher tax expenditures and tax evasion accounting for the larger part of the remainder. OECD estimates suggest that nearly two-thirds of the deficit overshoot was due to non-cyclical (both structural and temporary) factors (Diagram 12).

Official estimates attribute the largest shortfall to indirect taxes (Esc 215 billion or 2 per cent of GDP), followed by personal and corporate taxes

Table 10. **General government accounts**

National accounts basis

	1992 Latest estimated out-turn	1993 Budget	1993 Estimated out-turn	1994 Budget
	Billion escudos	Per cent rate of growth		
Current receipts	**4 969.1**	**7.6**	**0.0**	**6.7**
Per cent of GDP	43.7	44.1	41.7	41.9
Direct taxes	1 255.0	8.5	−4.5	4.4
Social contributions	1 306.9	11.6	10.4	4.1
Indirect taxes	1 777.9	10.5	−1.6	11.2
Other	629.3	−10.9	−7.9	4.5
Current expenditure	**5 084.8**	**5.3**	**6.9**	**5.2**
Per cent of GDP	44.7	44.2	45.6	45.1
Goods and services	2 063.6	8.6	6.0	5.9
Subsidies	158.1	21.5	16.2	7.7
Interest on debt	1 020.5	−6.2	−10.3	−11.7
Current transfers	1 842.7	6.8	16.5	11.5
Capital receipts	**430.4**	**−8.1**	**3.5**	**16.0**
Capital expenditure	**845.3**	**6.1**	**9.4**	**9.6**
Investment	487.8	6.0	8.6	19.8
Capital transfers and other	357.4	6.2	10.5	−4.1
Overall balance[1]	**−530.6**	**−511.7**	**−963.9**	**−907.0**
Per cent of GDP	−4.7	−4.2	−7.9	−7.2
Memorandum items:				
Non-interest expenditure	4 064.3	8.3	11.2	8.6
Primary balance[1]	489.9	445.3	−26.8	−99.1
Per cent of GDP	4.3	3.7	−0.2	−0.8
Total borrowing requirement[1]	−569.4	−562.8	−1 002.5	−942.3
Nominal GDP	11 366.0	6.7	4.9	6.2

1. Billion escudos.
Source: Ministerio das Finanças and OECD.

(Esc 163 billion). In addition to cyclical factors, the shortfall in direct taxes was caused by an overestimation of the 1992 tax base, which was negatively affected by the last quarter decline in GDP, and by the increased use by individuals and corporations of the generous opportunities for tax deductions that were granted following the 1989 tax reform. Although both domestic demand and imports were scheduled to rise in 1993, indirect tax revenues actually fell by around 1.5 per cent in 1993 from 1992 levels, suggesting a lack of effective enforcement

Diagram 12. **THE STANCE OF FISCAL POLICY**

Change in the cyclically-adjusted budget balance
(general government account)

% of GDP

% of GDP

Change in TOTAL balance

Change in PRIMARY balance

1990   91   92   93   94   95

Source: OECD estimates.

on the part of the tax administration. These problems have been compounded by the change in regime resulting from the harmonisation of value-added tax rates within the EC in 1993. While the standard rate dropped from 17 to 16 per cent, rates on a range of consumption goods were changed from 0 to 5 per cent, from 8 to 5 per cent and from 8 to 16 per cent. The Government seems to have overestimated the share of goods in private consumption subject to tax increases, leading to an overestimation of the revenue gains implied by tax harmonisation.[16] In addition, for a large importer such as Portugal, the elimination of border controls multiplied firms' opportunities for evading VAT on international transactions. Both tax evasion and tax avoidance may have been intensified by the slowdown of incomes due to the recession.

A supplementary budget was introduced in October 1993, aimed at cutting back both tax expenditures and tax evasion. Tax expenditures are to be curtailed by reducing deductions for rental payments and tightening discipline on deductions for branches of EC banks operating in Portugal. Tax loopholes are to be limited by reinforcing control over taxes on consolidated profits, eliminating tax exemptions for fixed asset revaluations, making controls on invoices at retail-sale level more stringent, and extending stamp duties (Imposto de selo) to international financial transactions.

Pressure on the debt ratio

Due to the larger general government borrowing requirement and the slow-down in GDP growth, the public debt ratio increased in 1993, for the first time since 1988, taking the debt ratio from 64 per cent in 1992 to about 67 per cent in 1993, according to government estimates (Diagram 13, panel A). As the public debt ratio began to rise and the economy slowed, the effective cost of debt service began to exceed nominal GDP growth by a significant margin (panel B). At the same time, sales of State assets decelerated and, following a change in the privatisation law, a smaller portion of proceeds was earmarked for debt buy-back. Due to heavy losses among the public enterprises, the use of privatisation proceeds to redeem debt is no longer compulsory. Proceeds earmarked for debt buy-back must account for at least 40 per cent, compared with a mandatory 80 per cent under the previous law.[17]

The deterioration in the public finances in 1993 has been such that failure to resume fiscal consolidation and to lower the cost of debt service could result in a spiral of interest and debt, jeopardising the medium-term sustainability of the fiscal stance. The seriousness of the fiscal situation is highlighted by the large medium-term "tax gap" that has opened up.[18] OECD estimates suggest that tax pressure would need to increase by 5 per cent of GDP over a five-year period in order to stabilise public debt at the 1993 level, given planned tax and spending policies and excluding privatisation proceeds.

With the overall debt level expanding, debt management policies continued to be directed at smoothing and lengthening the maturity structure of government liabilities and lowering their effective interest rate. The yield curve was extended from three to ten years as new markets for government securities were created. As a result, the share of medium-to-long-term bonds in total debt has doubled, from 8.4 per cent in 1992 to 15.9 per cent in 1993, while the share of short-term Treasury Bills has declined from 15 to 11 per cent. The average maturity has lengthened from 2.9 to 3.3 years. At the same time, the effective interest rate on government debt has fallen by 3 percentage points, from 14 to 11 per cent.[19]

Diagram 13. PUBLIC DEBT DEVELOPMENTS

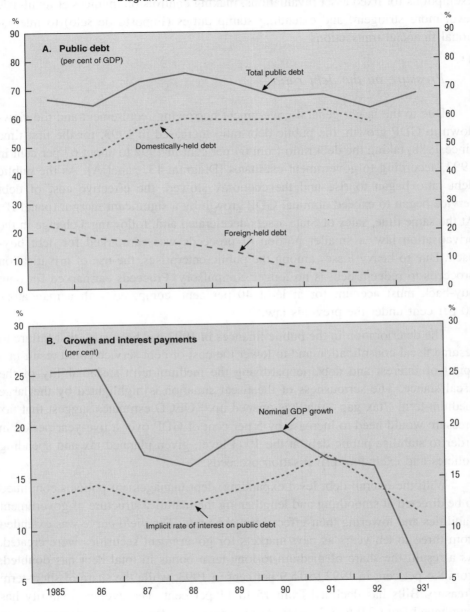

1. Estimates.
Source: OECD and Ministry of Finance.

The new medium-term convergence programme and the 1994 budget

The slowdown in economic activity and the 1993 fiscal slippage have prompted the government to modify its medium-term convergence programme, substantially relaxing both macroeconomic and fiscal targets (Table 11). Under the revised convergence programme, economic activity is projected to pick up slowly over the 1994-1997 period, with GDP growing at around 1.5 per cent in 1994 and inflation continuing to subside to the 3 to 4.3 per cent range by 1997. Based on these projections, the government plans to lower the general government deficit to slightly above 3 per cent of GDP, bringing the ratio of debt to GDP back to around 60 per cent by 1997. Since the contribution of the primary balance is expected to be small, deficit reduction is to be achieved mainly through a decline in interest payments. Despite the changes in the privatisation law noted above, debt stabilisation is expected to be speeded up by large privatisation proceeds, amounting to 1.4 per cent of GDP per year over the 1994-1997 period.

Underpinning the new medium-term convergence programme is a detailed Regional Development Programme (RDP), adopted in June 1993, which aims at lifting Portugal's per capita income from around 60 per cent to nearly 70 per cent

Table 11. Medium-term targets
Per cent of GDP

	QUANTUM (1990)	QUANTUM 2 (1992)	Modified QUANTUM 2 (1993)		
	1992-95	1993-95	1993	1994	1995-97
Fiscal targets[1]					
Overall balance[2]	4.5	3.0	−8.3	−7.0	−3.3
Primary balance	2.5	2.0	−0.5	−0.5	1.3
Public debt[3]	59.3	53.0	66.8	71.0	67.0
Macroeconomic targets					
GDP growth	3.8	4.0	0.0	1.5	3.5
Consumer price inflation	6.3	4.0-6.0	5.0-7.0	4.0-5.5	3.0-4.3

1. Administrative public sector, public accounts basis.
2. Excluding financial transactions.
3. Including debt buy-back with privatisation proceeds.
Source: Ministerio das Finanças.

of the EC average by 1999. Key factors in the catch-up process are employment and productivity gains based upon Community transfers, which, totalling 4.5 per cent of GDP over the 1995-99 period, are projected to raise real GDP growth by 0.5 percentage points a year over the next five years. Based upon the RDP, the second Community Support Framework (CSF), adopted in February 1994, targets human capital, infrastructure and the organisational know-how of small- and medium-sized enterprises as priority areas for investment. About 100 000 jobs would be created through these investments.[20]

Consistent with new medium-term programme, the Government aims at reducing the deficit-to-GDP ratio by about 1 percentage point in 1994 (Table 10). The return to fiscal restraint is to be achieved by means of a recovery of revenues, planned to grow at a rate 1.5 percentage points above the rate of growth of total expenditure. Apart from being dependent on cyclical recovery, the planned rise in tax revenues is based upon a set of fiscal measures contained in the 1994 Budget, intended to stabilise the ratio of revenues to GDP after the 1993 decline. Tax expenditures will be curtailed by raising the threshold for income tax deductions by less than the expected inflation rate, eliminating automatic tax allowances for housing maintenance, bringing taxes on old-age and disability pensions more in line with income taxation of dependent workers, and abolishing or lowering tax deductions for a number of saving plans.[21] In addition to steps taken in the Supplementary Budget, measures to combat tax evasion include changes in the fiscal regime covering mergers and tighter controls over financial transactions with "fiscal havens". Other revenue-raising measures include a 6 per cent increase in excise duties on commodities other than tobacco and cars and an increase in taxes on used cars.

On the other hand, the 1994 Budget reduces thresholds for VAT exemptions and more than offsets fiscal drag by widening income tax brackets by a margin in excess of expected inflation, thereby reducing the effective income tax rate. It also intends to modify the gasoline tax regime to facilitate price liberalisation in accordance with EC directives. On the spending side, the rise in total expenditures, which will be driven by increasing current transfers and public investment, is to be contained by continued restraint in public consumption and further declines in interest payments. For the third consecutive year, ceilings on nominal primary spending will be imposed, amounting to Esc 6.1 trillion for the general government and Esc 3.1 trillion for the state. As a result of these ceilings, which are only legally binding at the state level, current expenditures relative to GDP (excluding payments on account of the public employee pension fund) are planned to decline somewhat in 1994.[22] Consistent with this target, the government has proposed to keep nominal wages in the public sector flat in the context of the ongoing 1994 pay negotiations with trade unions. Savings in current spending will also result from the implementation of the pension reform voted in 1993. The social security reform increases the female retirement age from 62 to 65 years over a six-years period, lengthens the reference period used to compute base salaries, increases the number of contribution years needed to receive the maximum pension[23] and raises contribution rates for the liberal professions.

Greater recourse has been made to external finance, with external debt increasing from 4.8 per cent to 8.2 per cent of GDP in 1993. Efforts to smooth and extend the maturity structure of government debt will also continue in 1994. External public debt is planned to rise to 10 per cent of GDP and to stabilise thereafter. Foreign currency debt issues are viewed as a way to diversify risk and create benchmarks for investors. They may also constitute an effective way to abate the average cost of debt service to the extent that it proves possible to achieve relative stability of the escudo on foreign exchange markets. However, efforts will also be directed at reducing the risk premium on the domestic market. This risk premium is attributed both to fiscal considerations and to structural limitations of the domestic bond market. To overcome the latter problem, further measures have been proposed to promote the international integration of the Portuguese economy: double taxation of profits are to be abolished even for foreign branches of Portuguese companies operating in countries which have not signed bilateral agreements and, in a related move, the withholding tax on interest paid on external public debt is to be effectively scrapped by introducing a system under which non-residents are refunded within one day. Portugal currently levies a 20 per cent withholding tax on government bonds. While there are a number of double-taxation treaties for non-residents, the cumbersome and time-consuming reclaim procedure has led to an interest rate premium on Portuguese bonds over other markets.[24]

III. Promoting competition

Introduction

Since the beginning of the 1990s, consumer-price increases for non-trade-ables have exceeded those for tradeables by a significant margin.[25] In international terms this is not unusual, and, indeed, the disparity is not as marked in Portugal as in several other OECD economies (Table 12). However, both the size of this discrepancy and its persistence are novel phenomena for Portugal, pointing perhaps to structural impediments to the disinflation process. Widening to a record of 7 points in 1990 and narrowing to an estimated 4½ points in 1993, the inflation differential has naturally aroused concern among policy makers. Lack of disinflation momentum in the sheltered sector is widely seen as slowing down inflation convergence with the EC, a key objective of overall policies (Diagram 14).

Table 12. **Consumer prices for tradeables and non-tradeables**[1]

Percentage change

	Non-traded goods and services (per cent)	Traded goods (per cent)	Difference (percentage points)
Portugal	11.2	7.4	3.8
Germany (western)	5.5	2.7	2.8
France	4.5	1.6	2.9
Italy	7.5	2.8	4.7
United Kingdom	7.3	3.8	3.5
Belgium	4.2	2.4	1.8
Denmark	3.5	0.2	3.3
Greece	19.2	14.7	4.5
Spain	8.8	4.5	4.3
Ireland	3.9	2.5	1.4
Netherlands	4.1	2.6	1.5

1. 1992.
Source: Bank of International Settlements, *Annual Report 1992 of the Committee of EC Central Bank Governors.*

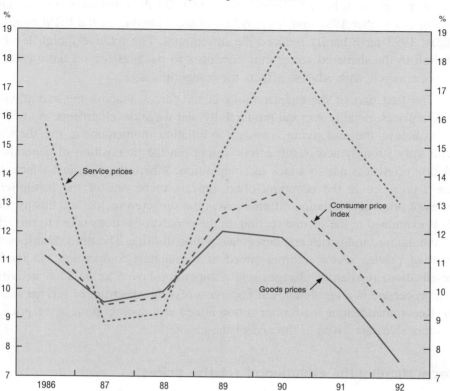

Diagram 14. **CONSUMER PRICE INFLATION**

Percentage change at annual rate

Source: Bank of Portugal (1993), *Report of the Board of Directors for the year 1992,* p. 86.

A major factor raising the terms-of-trade of non-tradeables has been macroeconomic: the shift in exchange rate policy which occurred in October 1990, when Portugal abandoned its 13-year old regime of small, pre-announced devaluations (''downward crawling peg''), allowing the escudo to float. The subsequent currency appreciation subjected price-setting in the exposed sector to increased discipline, which was reinforced by accession to the wider band of the ERM in April 1992. Indeed, nominal currency appreciation gathered speed until mid-1992, damping the rise in the prices of tradeables and pushing up the relative price of non-tradeables.[26] Thus, strengthening the exchange-rate regime and removing the last vestiges of capital controls in December 1992 have led to a new environment within which markets operate. On the other hand, the devaluations of November 1992 and May 1993 and the widening of the ERM bands in August 1993 have hardly reduced the differential. The relatively high level of inflation in the sheltered sector thus continues to put pressure on input costs in the open sector, with adverse effects for competitiveness.

The first part of the chapter looks at the forces shaping the evolution of relative prices, notably sectoral productivity and wage developments. As will be shown below, the underlying reasons for inflation momentum in the sheltered sector vary strongly across subsectors, ruling out the proposition of generalised inflation proneness due to a lack of competition. Where there is such a lack, the State's presence in the economy often appears to be one of the institutional causes of price- and inflation differentials in the sheltered sector, and this hypothesis is examined in the second section, in the context of actions taken to privatise the nationalised industries and deregulate public utilities. The third describes the extent of private sector reforms aimed at stimulating competition via market liberalisation, regulatory changes and competition-law reform. Such activities have proceeded in a highly uneven fashion across the spectrum of service activities. Recommendations for further action aimed at reducing the relative price of non-tradeables are given at the end of the chapter.

Forces shaping the evolution of relative prices

From a conceptual point of view, service-price inflation always tends to exceed goods-price inflation. Many service activities, including restaurants, hotels, teaching and social and other government services, have outputs which are very difficult to measure precisely or offer little or no scope for raising productivity.[27] In these subsectors, the level of labour productivity is often low, though in other services (financial, real estate, etc.) the opposite is true (Diagram 15). In general, if people holding jobs in the service sector are to enjoy increases in their standard of living, service output prices need to rise faster than goods prices (the so-called "relative price effect"). Moreover, the size of this relative price rise will tend to be larger for countries whose real incomes per head are rising fastest due to overall productivity improvement – which would be the case for an economy where incomes are catching up with those in mature economies (Diagram 16).

Diagram 15. **SECTORAL LABOUR PRODUCTIVITY LEVELS**[1]
Manufacturing = 100

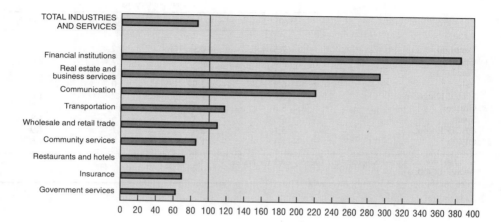

1. In 1991. Sectoral value added at 1985 prices, divided by employment.
Source: OECD, *National Accounts.*

Diagram 16. **THE RISE IN RELATIVE SERVICE PRICES**[1]
1985 = 100

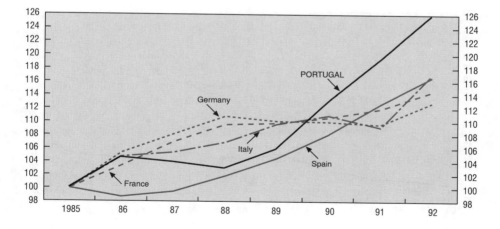

1. Index of consumer prices for services divided by index of consumer prices for goods.
Source: OECD.

51

Table 13.   **Productivity in the business sector**

Percentage changes at annual rates

	Labour productivity			
	1960 [1]-73	1973-79	1980-85	1986-92
Portugal	**7.5**	**0.5**	**0.2**	**2.6**
Germany	4.5	3.1	1.7	2.0
France	5.4	3.0	2.3	2.3
Italy	6.3	2.9	1.0	2.3
United Kingdom	3.6	1.6	3.2	1.0
Greece	8.8	3.3	0	1.9
Spain	6.0	3.3	3.6	1.8
OECD Europe	5.1	2.6	2.1	1.9
OECD	4.3	1.6	1.9	1.6

1.   1961 for the United Kingdom and Greece; 1963 for France; 1964 for Spain.
Source: OECD.

Diagram 17.   **REAL GDP PER CAPITA**[1]

United States = 100

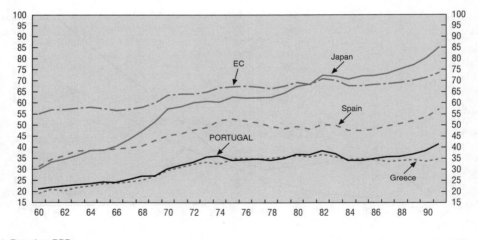

1. Based on PPPs.
Source: OECD, *National Accounts.*

52

Sectoral productivity trends

In fact, Portugal's overall productivity performance over the ten years to the mid-1980s was rather disappointing, considering its large catch-up potential: instead of outperforming high per-capita income countries, the country actually lagged behind in terms of labour productivity growth in the wake of the first oil price shock (Table 13). As a result, the process of real income convergence was reversed, contrasting with rapid progress made until the mid-1970s[28] (Diagram 17).

A more favourable picture emerges when attention is focused on developments in the second half of the 1980s. Mainly thanks to EC membership, productivity gains strengthened in both manufacturing and the sheltered sector, assisting the resumption of real income catch-up.[29] As would be expected, productivity advanced much less rapidly in the sheltered sector than in manufacturing (Diagram 18). Inside the protected sector, though, labour productivity trends in the 1980s diverged strongly. Exceptionally large productivity gains were recorded in transport and communication,[30] electricity, gas and water, exceeding those observed in manufacturing (Diagram 19). In finance, real estate and business services, labour productivity began to surge only in the second half of the 1980s, following Portugal's entry into the EC. Deregulation as well as organisational innovations and new technologies, associated with rising foreign investment, were main forces behind this development (see below). In contrast, productivity remained completely flat in the distribution sector, restaurants and hotels, a trend comparing unfavourably with developments in other countries.

Input costs

Cost developments also contributed to the relative inflation performance. In some sectors, notably distribution, strong labour cost growth reinforced weak or moderate advances in labour productivity, raising unit labour costs by large margins and feeding into prices (Diagram 20) (see below). In addition, costs of non-labour inputs, such as energy products and intermediate goods, after rising by more than 10 per cent in 1988, decelerated sharply and actually fell in absolute terms in 1991 and 1992. Services, being less energy-intensive than goods, benefitted less from such cost declines.[31]

53

Diagram 18. **LABOUR PRODUCTIVITY GROWTH IN THE SHELTERED AND OPEN SECTORS**

1980 = 100

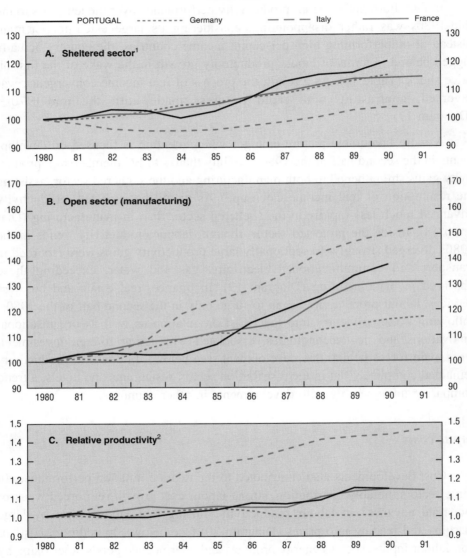

1. Including private and public services and construction.
2. Index of manufacturing productivity divided by index of productivity of sheltered sector.
Source: OECD, *National Accounts.*

Diagram 19. **SECTORAL LABOUR PRODUCTIVITY TRENDS**
1980 = 100

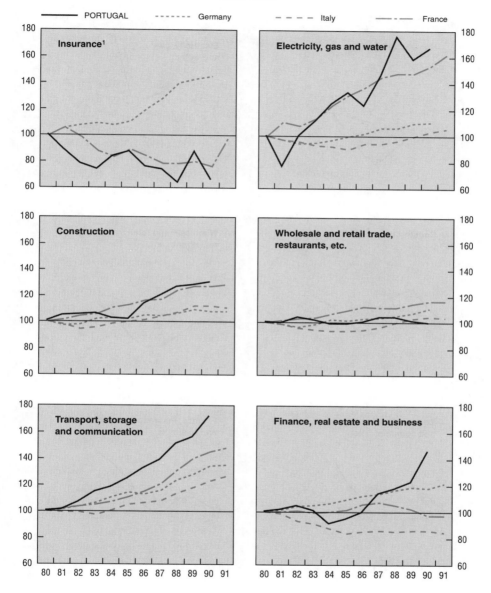

1. Not available for Italy.
Source: OECD, *National Accounts.*

Diagram 20. **TRENDS IN REAL COMPENSATION PER EMPLOYEE BY SECTOR**[1]

1980 = 100

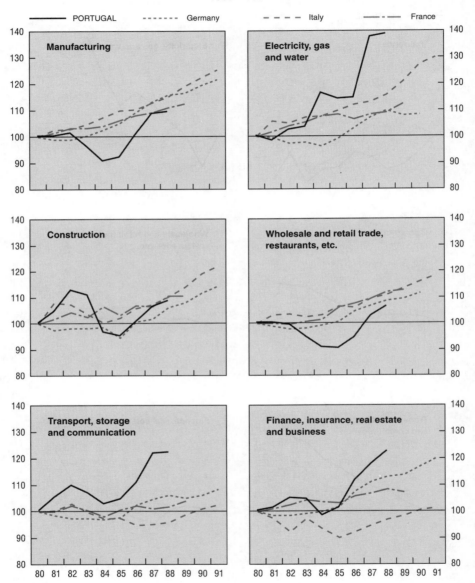

1. Compensation per employee deflated by the private consumption deflator.
Source: OECD, *National Accounts.*

Overall, empirical analysis shows a strong causality running from wage costs to output prices in Portugal's service sector, modified by productivity differences.[32]

- The rise in output prices in some labour-intensive sectors, such as wholesale and retail trades, restaurants and hotels, reflects the interaction of growing demand and weak productivity trends, due to limited scope for achieving efficiency gains, rather than competitive inadequacies (Diagram 21);
- Where output price inflation gathered speed in sectors with rapid productivity advances, such as communication, electricity and water supply and construction, lack of competition or over-regulation may have meant that the benefits to consumers have been reduced by wage pressures, or excess profits;
- In sectors where price increases were curbed by steep productivity gains, as in financial services, real estate and business services, heightened competition from deregulation may have acted to distribute the benefits more equally to producers and consumers.

These rather complex productivity, wage and price movements thus seem to have derived both from technological factors and from differences in the pace and extent of liberalisation and deregulation, which have meant that consumers have benefited more in some sectors than others.

Sectoral price levels

Despite the surge of service prices in 1989-90, prices for services rendered by restaurants, cafés and hotels were still only half the average EC level in 1990. Most other Portuguese prices were also relatively low, the comparison of OECD consumer price levels showing that Portugal had an overall 40 per cent price level advantage *vis-à-vis* the EC average, ranging from 60 per cent for education to 15 per cent for fuel and power (Diagram 22). The only major category suffering a significant price disadvantage has been purchases of personal transport equipment, reflecting high taxation and lack of skilled labour to repair cars and motorcycles.

Explanations of relatively high rates of inflation for services thus have to take account of their relatively low overall price level. This could be considered a

57

Diagram 21. **SECTORAL OUTPUT PRICE DEFLATORS**
Percentage change at annual rate

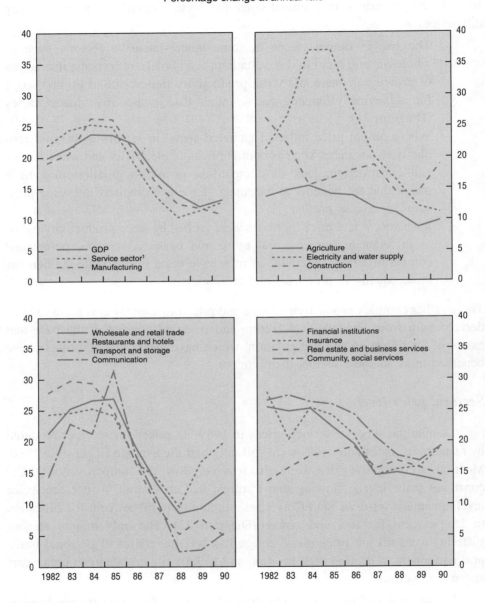

1. Excluding government.
Source: OECD, *National Accounts.*

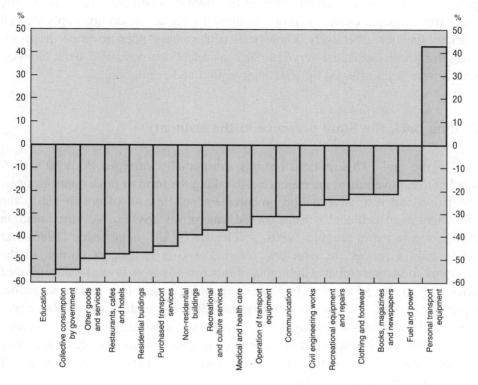

Diagram 22. **RELATIVE PRICE LEVELS[1] IN 1990
BETWEEN PORTUGAL AND THE EC**

1. Defined as the percentage difference between the price level in Portugal and the weighted average price level
   in EC countries
Source: OECD, Purchasing Power Parities and Real Expenditures.

normal feature for a country with a low per capita income. Portugal's position of having rather low service-sector prices relative to tradeables is consistent with international evidence suggesting relative service prices rise with national per capita income. However, the picture of relatively low prices *vis-à-vis* the EC average remains intact when price levels are scaled by per capita income levels based upon purchasing power parities (PPP). For each category of the sheltered sector, Portugal's position remains well below the regression line linking service price levels to income levels (see Annex). This suggests that some markets, particularly the labour market, may be functioning relatively efficiently. At the same time, though, comparatively low overall price levels do not imply that all markets function effectively. Other statistical sources point to price disadvantages for some individual services, such as telephone costs and bank charges, which have been affected by state intervention and regulation.

Rolling back the State presence in the economy

In the mid-1970s, nationalisations substantially enlarged Portugal's sheltered sector, government interference also taking the form of price controls, over-regulation and restrictive public procurement policies, all of which led to the inefficient management of State-owned enterprises (SOEs). A turnaround in policy orientation in the mid-1980s, accelerated by EC membership (1986), has set in train a process of structural reform, exposing a greater portion of the economy to market forces. Highlights of this process have been the decontrol of prices for goods and services (with few remaining exceptions) and privatisation. Despite extensive large-scale sell-offs started at the end of the 1980s, State-controlled companies in Portugal continue to exert a powerful impact on investment, output and employment. This implies that large segments of the economy are not subject to competitive pressures, exercised, for example, via the threat of bankruptcy and takeover bids.

Structural barriers to competition

In line with practice in other market economies, government regulation and intervention has typically been more pervasive in services than in manufacturing. According to the EC, sectors sheltered from competition until the establishment of the single European Market in 1993 included:[33]

- *Public procurement* markets such as telecommunications, energy-producing equipment, railway and other transport equipment as well as boilermaking, protected through limited access to public contracts; and industries protected by national standards and regulations including some food-processing, brewing and malting and shipbuilding. In the transport equipment sector the authorities have been the major customer

of national manufacturers. Here and in sectors such as boilermaking (for heating installations, power stations, refineries etc.) the protection afforded by the public procurement market is confirmed by low import penetration ratios and high relative prices.
- *Sectors with non-tariff barriers*, including footwear, textiles covered by the Multifibre Arrangement, motor vehicles imported from Japan and - for imports originating from certain non-OECD countries - a few other products.[34]

Although there is no sufficiently coherent source of information on technical standards to conclude whether these constitute an important barrier to entry, the public procurement and import penetration data suggest that relatively high prices in sectors such as telecommunications, energy and related investment-good industries - transport, electrical and non-electrical equipment - are a ttributable to pervasive State regulation and intervention. Finally, government purchases from the private sector as a percentage of general government consumption have been among the lowest in the OECD area, suggesting that competition has been inhibited. The share of less than 19 per cent in 1991-92 compares unfavourably with Germany (42 per cent), France (28 per cent), Italy (26 per cent) and Spain (21 per cent).[35]

Privatisation

Sales of public assets only became an integral part of structural reform in the second half of the 1980s, when a new policy orientation began to favour the play of competitive forces. Until then, three main categories of State-owned enterprises (SOEs) could be distinguished:
- Public enterprises created by a 1976 decree and placed under social ownership, which could not be transformed into private entities;
- Joint-stock companies in which the State owned the totality or the majority of shares. At the end of the 1980s, these companies accounted for no more than 5 per cent of total SOEs;
- Public financial holdings such as IPE - jointly owned by the Treasury, Cimpor, a state-owned cement company, the *Caixa Geral de Depósitos* and the *Banco de Fomento e Exterior* - and Partest. IPE has had

holdings in sectors deemed "strategic" such as automobiles, mechanical engineering,chemicals, biotechnology and, until 1992, telecommunications.

Prior to the adoption of the 1990 privatisation law, State-owned enterprises accounted for more than one-fifth of total value added in the non-agricultural business sector and more than one third of its total gross fixed investment, one of the highest shares among EC countries (Diagram 23). The employment share was, at 14 per cent, the largest after Italy and Greece. The State was still quasi-omnipresent in finance and insurance, the employment share of 95 per cent being by far the highest among EC countries, while it remained dominant in transport and communication (69 per cent) and energy and mining (57 per cent) (Table 14). Subsequent privatisation has substantially reduced the State's involvement in the economy. But panel data for 1990 put the SOEs' employment share at 9 per cent and their share in final sales at 12 per cent.

Efforts to roll back the State presence in the economy have so far concentrated on banks and insurance companies, leaving the SOEs a dominant influence in oil refining, shipbuilding, steel, cement and basic chemical products. Substantial losses marked the operations of many SOEs: in 1992, the combined borrowing requirements of non-financial SOEs totalled 1.5 per cent of GDP, largely reflecting losses made by the national oil company (*Petrogal*),[36] the state-owned steel company (*Siderurgia Nacional*), the petrochemical company (*Companhia Nacional de Petroquímica*), and the national airline (*TAP*).

The legal basis for the complete privatisation of nationalised firms[37] was laid down by a Constitutional Amendment of June 1989, which limited public majority ownership to strategic firms. Subsequent legislation, the privatisation law of 1990 (*Lei Quadro das Privatizações*), specified four main goals for State divestitures: raising Portugal's competitiveness; strengthening private entrepreneurship; developing capital markets and broadening share-ownership.

Under the 1990 privatisation law, foreign ownership was to be limited on a case-by-case basis, reflecting the authorities' intention of keeping large financial institutions under Portuguese control. This provision, which often amounted to a 25 per cent limit, however, was challenged by the EC for failing to give equal treatment to all investors from member countries and was abolished in early 1994. The original privatisation law also earmarked 80 per cent of privatisation

Diagram 23. **WEIGHT OF PUBLIC ENTERPRISES IN
THE NON-AGRICULTURAL BUSINESS SECTOR**

Percentage shares in 1990

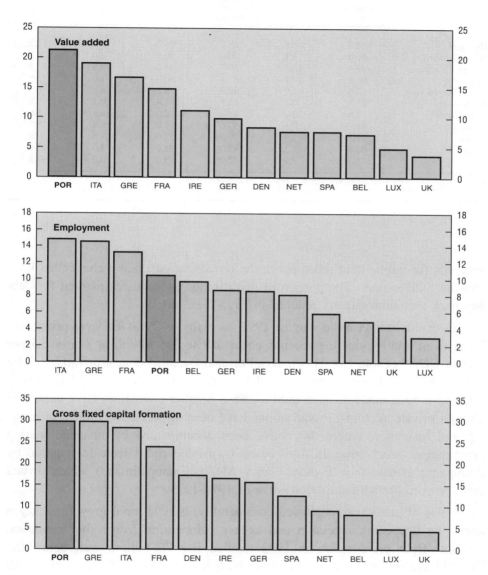

Note: Data for Germany and Italy refers to 1987 and 1988 respectively.
Source: CEEP (1994), *L'entreprise publique dans la Communauté européenne: Annales CEEP,* Brussels.

Table 14. **Weight of public enterprises in total employment by main branches of activity** [1]

Per cent

	Energy and mining	Industry	Transport and communication	Finance and insurance	Distribution	Total
Portugal	57.3	6.6	68.7	95.0	2.0	14.5
West Germany	60.0	1.1	70.0	30.6	2.0	8.8
France	78.5	12.7	59.0	34.0	2.8	13.3
Italy	85.4	10.1	81.4	50.0	1.0	15.8
United Kingdom	67.0	1.0	32.0	n.a.	n.a.	6.0
Belgium	23.7	0.1	63.5	8.4	0.1	9.8
Netherlands	2.0	2.2	43.7	2.0	n.a.	6.0
Denmark	88.0	0.5	57.6	1.0	n.a.	8.5
Ireland	71.3	1.4	79.7	32.0	1.8	10.7
Greece	62.0	1.3	45.0	31.0	3.0	15.0
Spain	41.0	3.7	32.0	3.0	0.2	7.5

1. Non-agricultural business sector employment, 1988.
Source: CEEP (1990), *L'entreprise publique dans la Communauté européenne: Annales CEEP*, Brussels.

proceeds for public debt redemption, the remaining part being channelled back into the SOE system. The portion of privatisation proceeds earmarked for debt buy-back was subsequently reduced in 1993 (see Part II).

Over the four years to August 1993, as many as 29 SOEs were privatised, 21 of them totally, yielding receipts equal to Esc 736 billion or nearly 6.5 per cent of GDP[38] (Table 15). This makes Portugal the third largest privatiser in the OECD, after the United Kingdom and New Zealand. In the case of large firms, sales have been made through public offers. Smaller companies have been sold through private auctions. Privatisations have been largely concentrated in banking and insurance, where they have been accompanied by financial market deregulation (see below). In most cases, ownership rights were re-acquired by Portuguese groups (*e.g.* Espírito Santo, Mello, Champalimaud) which owned them prior to the nationalisation wave of 1974-1975.[39]

Sales of public assets slowed considerably in 1993 amid growing concern about the deepening recession and keener competition from other countries. Receipts from privatisation in 1993 totalled Esc 76 billion, well below the Esc 225 billion specified by the 1993 budget law. Many of the firms which remain to be privatised are in ailing sectors, including the chemical, steel and airline industries. The full sale of the steel company *Siderurgia Nacional*, ini-

Table 15. **Major privatisations, 1989-1993**

Enterprise	Date	Percentage sold	Method	Total revenue (in million escudos)	Sector
Banco Totta & Açores (first tranche)	10.07.89	49.0	Public offer	285 794	Banking
Tranquilidade (first tranche)	04.12.89	49.0	Public offer	257 775	Insurance
BTA (second tranche)	31.07.90	31.0	Public offer	223 552	Banking
Centralcer	12.11.90	100.0	Public offer	345 851	Food/beverages
Banco Português Atlantico (first tranche)	11.12.90	33.0	Public offer	497 527	Banking
Banco Espiritu Santo (first tranche)	09.07.91	40.0	Public offer	608 661	Banking
Banco Fonseca Burnay	27.08.91	80.0	Public tender	360 800	Banking
Banco Espiritu Santo (second tranche)	25.02.92	60.0	Public offer	890 176	Banking
Banco Português Atlantico (second tranche)	25.05.92	17.64	Public tender	506 250	Banking
Petrogal	04.06.92	25.0	Public tender	408 000	Oil
Imperio	17.11.92	100.0	Public offer	255 122	Insurance
CPP	12.12.92	100.0	Public offer	408 241	Insurance
União Bancos Português	13.02.93	61.0	Public offer	244 194	Banking
Banco Português Atlantico (third tranche)	07.07.93	17.5	Public offer	323 749	Banking

Source: Data supplied by the Portuguese authorities.

Diagram 24. **PLANNED PRIVATISATIONS IN EUROPE**
US$ billion

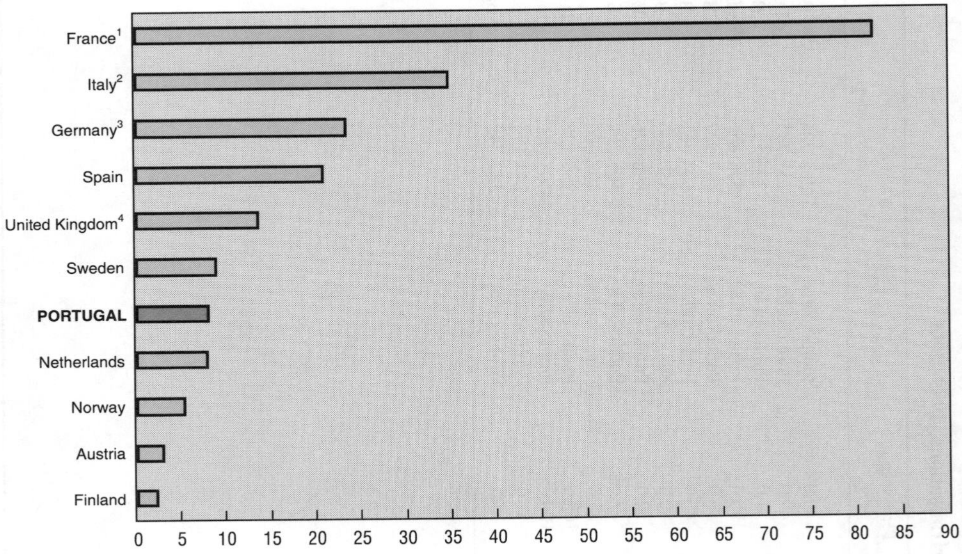

1. Excludes CNP and Bull.
2. Excludes Crediop, IMI, INA, Ilva and Iritecna.
3. Excludes Treuhand.
4. Excludes British Coal.
Source: Morgan Stanley Research (June 1993) and Portuguese authorities.

tially due in the second half of 1993, may be delayed until the end of the 1990s, depending upon the approval by the EC of restructuring plans. Other deferred privatisations concern *Portucel*, a pulp and paper group and the second-largest Portuguese exporter, and the cement groups *Secil* and *Cimpor*. Privatisation receipts during the period 1993-97 are projected to yield $8 billion (Diagram 24).

Deregulation of public utilities

While government intervention may often be justified by market failure, pressure from interest groups has tended to maintain and reinforce regulations beyond the point needed to correct for market imperfections.[40] In Portugal, as in many other OECD economies, the recipe has often been for public utilities' prices to be controlled and kept artificially low, while at the same time protecting employment. Using public service companies for purposes of short-term macroeconomic stabilisation of both prices and employment has led to suppressed inflation, to distorted relative prices and to suboptimal investment decisions. As regards public utilities, their liberalisation and restructuring is still at an early stage. However, in some instances, such as in transport, electricity and telecommunications, deregulation has gone hand in hand with the adoption of new technology, bolstering productivity.

The foundation for restructuring and liberalising the telecommunication sector was laid by the legislation passed in 1989 (*Lei de Base das Telecomunicações*). While the provision of basic telecommunications services continues to be under government ownership, as in most other countries,[41] complementary and value-added services can now be supplied by any individual or legal entity. As a result, competition in non-core subsectors has intensified, *e.g.* in mobile telecommunications where a private consortium endowed with a concession started operating in 1992. In this sector, the rise in competition is likely to take place in a rapidly expanding market, the number of "mobile subscriptions" being low by EC standards (Table 16). On the other hand, costs for placing telephone calls remain among the highest in the EC, after Spain and Italy.

Table 16. **Telecommunications indicators**[1]

	Lines per 100 population	Monthly costs in capital city (US$)[2]	International outgoing traffic (millions of minutes)	Mobile subscriptions ('000)	Annual average cost (US$)[3]
Portugal	27.3	2 105	139	12.6	1 313
Germany	41.6	1 652	3 557	532.5	2 365
France	51.0	1 171	2 182	290.0	2 242
Italy	40.4	2 119	1 341	568.0	1 151
United Kingdom	44.6	906	248	130.0	1 028
Greece	41.7	1 669	719	14.3	..
Spain	35.3	2 355	..	108.5	1 381

1. 1991.
2. Connection, rental and user charges for 2 000 minutes per month of telephone calls.
3. Monthly fee and 90 minutes per month of peak-time calls plus 60 minutes per month of off-peak-time calls.
Source: Lehman Brothers; International Telecommunications Union; Inteldata Ltd.; Autorità Garante per la Concorrenza e il Mercato (Italy).

As part of a legal restructuring, shares owned by the State in *Correios e Telecomunicações de Portugal* (CTT) were transferred in 1992 to a newly created public holding company, *Comunicações Nacionais* (CN), itself divided into five separate operating companies:

- *CTT-Correios de Portugal* for postal services;
- *Telefones de Lisboa e Porto* (TLP) operating the public network in greater Lisbon and greater Oporto;[42]
- *Telecom* for the rest of the country and European telecommunications;
- CPRM (*Companhia Portuguesa de Radio Marconi*), 51 per cent owned by the State, holds a concession to operate intercontinental services via submarine cable and satellite until 2001;
- TDP (*Teledifusora de Portugal*).

The legal structure of the telecommunications industry is likely to be modified further, as three companies, operating in different segments of the markets, seem unable to meet the rising demand for a better quality of telecommunication services:[43] the average waiting period for a new connection is close to two months, substantially longer than in other EC countries. Privatisation could potentially remedy this defect, and the approach currently pursued is one of creating a new company (*Portugal Telecom*), resulting from the merger of TLP, Telecom and TDP. The government intends to restrict the initial disposal to between 20 and 30 per cent with a view to forming a core of domestic investors. Under an agreement with the EC, full liberalisation of telecommunications is only due for 2003, five years later than for other member countries.

Some progress has also been made in strengthening competitive forces in electricity generation and distribution. The full implementation of the EC directive giving access to third-party producers will eventually allow energy to be traded without restrictions imposed by monopolies. For final users, some measure of flexibility has been introduced into the pricing system in October 1993. Providing a greater differentiation of charges, the new tariff structure has significantly lowered electricity prices for industrial users.

The government's objectives are to introduce private financing into the expansion of the system. Accordingly, a joint venture between Portuguese private interests and other European investors was awarded a concession to build, buy and operate the Pego coal-fired power plant, due to provide one tenth of

Portugal's electricity needs. The first unit at the plant came into commercial service in early 1993, the second being scheduled to come on stream in early 1995. A recent EC decision restricted to fifteen years the period in which *Electricidade de Portugal*, the State-owned monopoly, will have exclusive rights to electricity produced by the Pego plant. Challenging a 28-year exclusive agreement, the EC argued that a supply obligation for a period of over 15 years was a restrictive practice and constituted therefore a trade distortion. Development of subsequent units at Pego may follow the planned addition of natural gas units. Legislation passed in August 1993 called for the creation of an independent regulator for the gas sector, though the authority of the regulator has yet to be defined. Similarly, the government is considering the establishment of an independent regulator for the electricity sector.

In air transport, TAP, the State-owned national carrier, lost its monopoly rights over scheduled international flights in 1989, when a private firm (*Portugalia*) began serving various European cities.[44] From 1993, some foreign carriers have taken advantage of the first phase of EC-wide liberalisation, allowing them to take passengers on the "intra-Portugal leg" of international flights. However, the fact that TAP's operating losses in 1993 totalled Esc 35 billion, the worst result in the company's history, testifies to the need for greater operating efficiency in the airline sector.

Strengthening competitive forces in the private sector

Privatisation and public utility deregulation have gone hand in hand with the adoption of measures to expose the private sector to rising competitive pressure, with beneficial effects on labour productivity. In the banking sector, for example, efficiency gains made employers more inclined to grant generous pay increases (Diagrams 19 and 20).[45] Foreign direct investment attracted by market derestriction has been a catalyst for the diffusion of process and product innovations.[46] In banking alone, such investment amounted to 1.5 per cent of GDP a year, on average, in the 1986-92 period. For the economy as a whole, the ratio was 2.7 per cent, sharply up from 0.7 per cent in the 1975-85 period.[47]

Deregulation of financial markets

Financial market deregulation began in 1984, gathering pace after accession to the EC.[48] In the process, credit ceilings were abolished, deposit rates freed, restrictions on opening bank branches eased, returns on financial claims against the public sector brought to market levels and controls on capital inflows and outflows removed. In addition, the system of compulsory reserves was extended to all financial intermediaries collecting short-term funds, including investment banks and leasing and factoring firms.[49]

A new banking law, passed in December 1992, unified the various pieces of legislation relevant to bank supervision while the 1993 budget law terminated the Treasury's overdraft facility at the Bank of Portugal. The new banking law also provided a framework for Portugal's banking system to shift to universal banking, under which banks are allowed to participate in both commercial and investment business. Banks were also allowed to begin factoring and leasing activities as of January 1993. Applying the principle of home country control, as required by the second EC directive, the law stipulated that all banks operating in Portugal are supervised by the central bank of the home country. As allowed by the EC, liquidity control and regulation of risk exposure remain in the domain of Portuguese authorities. The new banking law also laid out a framework for establishing a deposit insurance scheme in line with the EC's draft Deposit Protection Directive, which incorporates the principle of home country deposit insurance.[50]

The number of banks operating in Portugal more than doubled between 1983 and 1992, rising from 16 to 35. Thanks to computerised techniques and low overhead costs, private banks have rapidly gained market shares at the expense of overstaffed and undercapitalised State-owned banks. While the number of nationalised banks fell to 7, that of foreign banks climbed from 3 to 15 in the same period, testifying a strong foreign presence.[51] Bank branches more than tripled between 1983 and 1992, pushing the ratio of the number of branches to population far above the EC average.[52] Privatisation opened the door for a significant restructuring.[53] Despite mergers, however, Portuguese banks remain small by European standards (Table 17).

Intermediation margins, as measured by the spread between bank lending and deposit rates, have narrowed over time, but continue to be large by international comparison, revealing a persistent competitive disadvantage. Portuguese

Table 17. **The top 500 European banks**

Ranking by capital base at end December 1992 or March 1993

	Total	Top 100	101-200	201-300	301-400	401-500
Portugal	11	2	5	3	1	0
Germany	93	19	20	14	20	20
France	26	12	3	5	2	4
Italy	104	20	18	21	20	25
United Kingdom	35	10	5	8	8	4
Greece	8	1	3	3	2	0
Spain	47	8	12	11	10	6

Source: The Banker, September 1993.

bank charges continue to be among the highest in Europe, partly because of the stamp tax and the high reserve coefficient.[54] Moreover, even though the number of employees per banking branch fell to the EC average in the early 1990s, overall efficiency, as measured by the number of credits per bank employee, has remained low by EC standards. On the other hand, a recent study found strong competitive pressure in the market for bank loans, with risk premia largely accounting for the spread among bank lending rates in different niches of the market.[55]

As part of capital market reform, the government privatised the Lisboa and Porto Stock Exchanges in 1991, and established a supervisory agency (*Comissão de Mercado de Valores Mobiliarios*) and a central clearing house. A continuous trading system was also introduced. At the same time, privatisations of State-owned companies have raised the number of shareholders, but these, at only 2 per cent of the population, remain few compared with other EC countries.

Notwithstanding rapid growth, Portugal's insurance market has remained the smallest in the EC, accounting for only 0.2 per cent of total EC life insurance premia in 1989 and 0.8 per cent of non-life insurance premia.[56] This partly reflects the low ratio of cars to population.[57] Life insurance density, as measured by premia per capita expressed in US dollars, quintupled in the second half of the 1980s, but remained a fraction of the EC average. The gap is smaller for the density of non-life insurances.

On the supply side, the number of insurance firms has nearly doubled since 1987, but at 95, Portuguese insurance companies represent little more than 0.1 per cent of the EC total. On the other hand, market concentration has been high, with the top 10 direct insurance companies controlling nearly 90 per cent of the insurance business in 1989.[58] Strong concentration may in part be responsible for low efficiency: in 1988, the level of labour productivity, measured by the value of gross direct premia per employee, was still less than one fourth of the EC average. Also, productivity trends for insurance companies weakened during the 1980s, contrasting with surging productivity gains in the banking sector (Diagram 19).

Finally, private pension funds are still underdeveloped compared with other countries, partly reflecting the generosity of the basic social security scheme.[59] Under the 1993 pension reform, the basic benefit is calculated as a proportion of average earnings in the best ten of the fifteen years preceding retirement. For a person earning approximately the average wage, this would correspond to about 70 per cent of pay, a relatively high replacement level. Even so, in terms of GDP total pension payments rank among the lowest in the EC, partly a consequence of demographic factors. Fully-funded private schemes established after 1987 are required to be managed on a segregated basis by investment institutions (*sociedades gestoras de fundos de pensões*) authorised by the Ministry of Finance on the advice of the Institute of Insurance. The 1987 legislation also requires new pension funds to be of the defined-benefit type.

Retail trade liberalisation

Small, family-owned shops dominate Portugal's retail trade. Accounting for roughly two fifths of total sales, twice the EC average, these shops are far more important than in any other EC country.[60] However, in the early 1990s, larger establishments have strongly expanded their market share, especially in the food domain. In this market, sales by hypermarkets surged from 11.7 per cent of total sales in 1988 to 30.9 per cent in 1992, putting Portugal in the fourth place in the EC after France, the United Kingdom and Spain.

A new law, due to take effect in 1994, will ease restrictions governing the creation of new retail outlets. Requirements for issuing new licences are more restrictive at the national than at the regional level. Thus, by raising the threshold beyond which regulatory competences pass from the regional to the national level, the new law could lower entry barriers.[61]

Beginning in the early 1980s, price controls and price surveillance for most goods were reduced in steps,[62] and the public display of prices was made mandatory. Gasoline prices were decontrolled in 1993, although a ceiling remains in force until 1994. The 1993 amendments to the retail trade law open the door for further liberalisation. In addition, a government programme aims at smoothing the transition to a more competitive retail trade system.

Liberalisation of the housing market

For resident property rented before 1985, current legislation provides almost a life security of tenure without any open-market rent reviews. For property rented after 1985, legislation allows fixed five-year contracts to be signed. As a result, about 80 per cent of all rents paid are below the market level, many well below because of the rent freeze which operated up to 1985. Rent adjustments are presently based upon increases in consumer prices, with specific increases linked to significant housing improvements. In conjunction with the distortions to the property and inheritance tax systems caused by the undervaluation of older properties, the regulatory framework thus continues to discriminate against new building investment, leading to a growing shortage of residential and office property.

Competition policy

Portugal's first law on competition, introduced in 1983, sought to prevent harmful effects from collusive behaviour and abuse of market power. It also aimed at suppressing individual practices hindering competition, such as setting minimum prices or refusing to sell goods or services. In the early 1990s, three further pieces of legislation were passed to improve the general framework in which markets operate:

- the bankruptcy law of 1992 eased the previously severe restrictions impeding the dissolution of firms;
- a decree-law on public procurement of 1993 strengthened the application of fair practices in the bidding for public contracts;

- a new competition law of January 1994 tightened the definition of abuse of dominant position and reinforced the legal response to restrictive practices, while maintaining the basic provisions of the 1983 legislation.

The new decree-law on public procurement introduces new procedures to screen applicants for public tenders, reducing the scope for discriminatory adjudication. It also restricts special cases for which private negotiations are allowed. Finally, the Minister of Trade and Tourism, who is also in charge of competition surveillance (see below), will join the Ministers of Public Works and Finance in taking decisions.

Motivated by the rapid pace of structural change and inspired by EC regulations, the new competition law, which came into force on 1 January 1994, widens the scope of application of the old law, while maintaining its basic provisions. The law applies to all economic activities undertaken in the public, private and cooperative sector, whether lasting or temporary. Exempt from the law are enterprises subject to special legislation, e.g. public utilities and their monopoly rights. It also incorporates and strengthens the procedures for merger control established by a separate law in 1988. Mergers among credit institutions, finance and insurance companies are subject to special supervision by the Bank of Portugal and the Insurance Institute.

The new competition law goes beyond the principle of abuse of dominant position, embodied in the previous 1983 legislation, by introducing the concept of "state of economic dependence". Under the previous legislation, vertical restraints imposed by suppliers on dependent clients were considered a restriction on competition only when practised by firms holding a dominant position in a good or service market. Thus, an undertaking wielding economic power, but not holding a dominant position in the market, could escape investigations of the Directorate General for Competition and Prices (DGCP) of the Ministry for Trade and Tourism. The new law is more restrictive in prohibiting all abuses of economic dependence, irrespective of the firm's market position. On the other hand, it does not forbid those restrictive practices which enterprises use to increase their competitiveness.[63]

In conformity with EC regulations, the scope of merger control has been widened and interpretative difficulties eased. A prior notification of mergers is required when the resulting firm either controls 30 per cent or more of the

74

domestic market in specific goods or services, or has a turn-over in Portugal exceeding Esc 30 billion. The law also addresses the problem of aid provided by the State or by any other public body: assistance must not restrict or have a significant effect on competition in any market or segment of it.

Investigative powers continue to be exercised by the DGCP, which employs 160 persons, partly for the purpose of price data collection. Under the 1994 law, the Directorate had the power to initiate investigations, enjoying the same rights and being subject to the same duties as the police. Findings in most cases are transmitted to the Council for Competition for final decision. The Council is an independent body headed by either a judge or an officer from the Public Legal Service, and is composed of four or six voting members, appointed by the Prime Minister. Until 1993, about 100 cases of restrictive practices had been examined by the competition authority, of which 60 were referred to the Council. Sanctions were imposed upon 40 firms. A total of 54 merger cases have also been examined so far, with only one of them viewed as deleterious to competition.

The scope for further action

While the array of measures aimed at deregulating and liberalising the economy has been impressive, in order to sustain the pace of real income and inflation convergence it seems imperative to increase the momentum of reform and broaden its approach. The banking sector, though benefiting from large foreign direct investment, still lags behind most other EC countries in terms of efficiency, adding to input costs in the exposed sector. The insurance sector, judging by its trend decline in productivity and high concentration, needs over-hauling. A web of restrictions hangs over the housing market, depressing investment.

An area of special concern is the public utilities. Natural monopolies in electricity, water, mail, transport and telecommunications involve a well-known conflict between productive efficiency and the exercise of monopoly power, which may distort relative prices and reduce consumer welfare. Introducing market discipline via privatisation may have little influence on efficiency in these cases, since the size of firms and veto powers retained by the government after privatisation make take-overs unlikely. Injecting greater competition at the same time as the change in ownership is therefore necessary to stimulate efficiency.[64] The room for doing so has widened over time:

- In some cases, the removal of barriers to entry and the ensuing market contestability may improve the internal economic efficiency of the public utilities, although contestability may not prove strong enough to eliminate monopoly power;
- To some extent, competition for the market in the form of franchising can be a substitute for direct state control and a valid supplement to regulation of certain public services;
- In many cases, technological innovations have invalidated economies of scope as justification for public service provision. This is true, for instance, for some mail and telecommunications services.

While welfare gains from derestriction and privatisation are closely dependent upon the redesign of the regulatory framework, optimality criteria are controversial and various approaches have been attempted in OECD countries.[65] However, since economies of scale and sunk costs appear to be related more to distribution networks than to production itself, competitive forces could be strengthened by forcing utilities to split their businesses between production and the access to the distribution network. This can be achieved either by breaking up the public monopoly position[66] or by establishing separate accounts for each activity.

Overall, the scope for lifting productivity levels through deregulation and structural reform in the sheltered sector is still large. Exploiting this potential would assist Portugal in its efforts to achieve real income convergence. However, it is also apparent from the relatively disappointing overall productivity growth of the economy that inflation performance could be improved by determined efforts to strengthen productivity and upgrade human capital in the economy at large. This not only requires granting wider access to higher education but also greater emphasis on stimulating R&D efforts. Following this path has become all the more important since competition from eastern and central Europe for inward direct investment has grown, raising prospects of a reduced inflow of organisational and technological know-how from abroad.

IV. Conclusions

Portugal's economy slipped into recession in early 1993, leaving GDP for the year around ½ per cent lower than in 1992, the worst growth outcome in nine years. Unemployment began to rise sharply, albeit from low levels. Reflecting Portugal's highly flexible labour market, nominal wage growth fell, enabling consumer-price inflation in 1993 to remain a little below the upper band of the 5 to 7 per cent target range. However, the effects of currency depreciation were increasingly felt in the second half, as faster price rises for tradeables dominated a continued moderation of unit labour costs. At over 6 per cent in December 1993, consumer-price inflation still exceeded the EC average by more than 3 points. On the external side, a change in statistical procedures prevents a direct comparison with 1992. However, it is estimated that the trade deficit contracted in 1993, shifting the current account into surplus.

With unit labour costs decelerating, export market growth picking up and interest rates trending down, the economic expansion should resume in 1994 and quicken thereafter. Helped by a growing surplus in invisibles trade, the current account surplus may widen in 1994. With output growth below potential, the rate of unemployment may continue to rise to nearly 7 per cent in 1995, further assisting the disinflation process. But the expected rise in consumer prices seems set to remain above 5 per cent in 1994 according to OECD projections, due both to the lower value of the escudo and to persisting inflation in the sheltered sector. The projections thus suggest a slowing in the rate of inflation convergence with Portugal's EC partners, which has been the central aim of economic policy since 1987.

The primary intermediate target by which convergence was to be achieved has been exchange rate stability. However, the credibility of this commitment came under renewed strain in 1993 as the escudo was exposed to repeated waves of downward pressure, culminating in a devaluation in the context of the May

1993 realignment. This was the second parity change in the escudo within six months. Exchange rate tensions were linked initially to general exchange rate turbulence, including pressures on the Spanish peseta, but also stemmed increasingly from the difficulty of maintaining a sufficiently tight monetary stance at a time when external demand was weakening and Portuguese exporters were suffering squeezed profit margins. In a cyclical environment where the flexibility of the monetary authorities to raise interest rates was limited to some extent, and where the policy mix was becoming increasingly unbalanced because of fiscal slippage, confidence in the credibility of stabilisation policies was eroded.

Following the devaluation, the Portuguese authorities have reasserted the primacy of the stable exchange rate objective. Despite the widening of the ERM bands in August, the escudo has continued to trade within the old rate band. The risks of currency turmoil seem to have subsided with the widening of the bands, and the interest rate differential with Germany was broadly stable until early 1994. Thereafter, interest rate convergence resumed, indicating a greater investor confidence in the Portuguese monetary stance. Overall, short-term interest rates eased by more than 4 points between August 1992 and early 1994. But in February they were still 4 points higher than in Germany, a differential which is only slightly lower than that observed in the summer of 1992. Thus the risk premium on escudo instruments has remained substantial. Restoring credibility and reducing the premium will require a better balanced policy mix, based on a continued firm monetary stance and backed up by fiscal stringency. Market expectations should then stabilise, preventing a slide of the escudo within the wider band. The cost of such a policy in terms of output foregone would be damped by the high degree of real wage flexibility which characterises Portugal's labour market.

The large fiscal deficit is one of the key factors preventing a more rapid convergence in Portuguese interest rates to EC levels. The 1991 convergence programme originally aimed at halving the general government budget deficit to 3 per cent by 1995, with a lowering of the public debt ratio to 55 per cent. Instead, the budget deficit was allowed to soar to nearly 8 per cent of GDP in 1993, rendering the original targets unattainable. Relative to initial budget proposals, the deficit overshoot in 1993 was around 3½ per cent of GDP, pushing up public debt to close to 70 per cent of GDP. This slippage has been due, in part, to cyclical factors: the descent into recession would have been steeper, had the authorities not allowed the automatic stabilisers to operate. Unfortunately, however, the jump in the budget deficit far exceeded what can be attributed to the widening of cyclical slack. According to OECD estimates, as much as 60 per cent of the rise in the budget deficit was due to the once-for all effect of lost VAT revenue and other non-cyclical forces which could represent an underlying reversal of the fiscal consolidation process.

The deficit problem seems not to have emanated from the spending side, where, despite higher social security transfers, the aim of keeping non-interest expenditure within a nominal ceiling was largely met for the second consecutive year. It has derived principally from a shortfall in revenues from VAT and the corporate tax, reflecting, in addition to cyclical factors, tax avoidance and evasion as well as errors in estimating the revenue impact of VAT harmonisation. Thus, while the newly introduced system designed to monitor State expenditure has been relatively successful in improving government spending controls, substantial leakages opened up on the revenue side. These demand immediate remedy. In particular, the shortfall in VAT receipts suggests that administrative measures are needed to prevent tax evasion, while tax loopholes in the income tax system, which make tax avoidance too easy and tax-expenditures difficult to contain, should be closed. In addition, the errors made in calculating the tax base for 1993 underline the urgent need for measures to upgrade the capacity of the tax administration to provide more timely data which would make it possible for the authorities to base budget proposals upon more realistic revenue assumptions.

To restore confidence in the convergence process after the 1993 deficit overrun it is imperative to establish a renewed commitment to fiscal retrenchment. A truly improved mix between fiscal and monetary policy would calm market apprehensions, reducing inflation expectations and opening up opportunities for further interest rate cuts. Conversely, any failure to resume fiscal consolidation would jeopardise medium-term policy credibility, endangering the convergence of inflation and interest rates to European levels and risking a spiral of interest payments and debt accumulation. In recognition of this, the new medium-term convergence programme, presented with the 1994 Budget, and endorsed at ministerial level by the European Union in February 1994, envisages a cut in the fiscal deficit to 3.3 per cent of GDP within the 1995 to 1997 period. This will be based upon continued expenditure restraint and new measures aimed at rolling back tax evasion, and will be assisted by the proceeds of further privatisations.

Public debt is expected to resume its downward trend in 1995 in terms of GDP. However, no primary budget surplus is expected until 1995 at the earliest and about two-thirds of the improvement on the spending side comes from the assumption of lower interest charges. These assumptions could prove optimistic. Hence, while the 1994 budget is a step in the right direction, further fiscal action may be needed if the markets are to be convinced of the authorities' determination to keep budgetary developments on track.

Achieving inflation convergence over the medium term also depends on action being taken to open up further the sheltered sector of the economy, where the disinflation process has so far been slower than in manufacturing. Structural reforms dating from the policy reorientation of the mid-1980s, prompted by EC membership, have exposed a rising portion of the economy to market forces. The public stake in the business sector has shrunk significantly, while prices for most goods and services have been decontrolled, restrictions on capital movements removed and financial markets substantially liberalised. More recent measures include new legislation on bankruptcy (1992), banking (1993), public procurement (1993), and competition (1994), all aimed at harmonising Portuguese laws with EC competition and regulation directives. Despite the progress made, however, price and inflation patterns suggest that, while the efficiency of the labour market helps to keep the overall cost of services internationally rather low, large segments of the service-producing economy are still not sufficiently subject to competitive pressures.

The pace of deregulation and privatisation has been fastest in financial markets. Direct monetary control ended with the abolition of credit ceilings and restrictions on interest rates, allowing returns on financial claims, especially those against the State which were formerly controlled, to reach market levels. In addition, the authorities extended the system of compulsory reserves to include all financial intermediaries and eased restrictions on opening bank branches. As a result, foreign direct investment in banking surged in the 1986-92 period, the number of banks more than doubling over the last ten years and banking productivity growing strongly. Nevertheless, the financial sector still lags behind most other EC countries in terms of efficiency, adding to business costs. Although reduced, financial intermediation margins remain large by international comparison, calling for further action to enhance competition.

The reforms already taken in banking and finance stand in contrast to inadequate progress made in introducing competition in other areas, including housing, insurance, public transport, public utilities, notably electricity and water, and, more generally, the restructuring of ailing state-owned companies (such as steel and chemicals). Severe restrictions continue to beset the housing market, keeping about 80 per cent of all rents paid below market levels and depressing maintenance spending and investment. The insurance industry, judging by its trend decline in productivity and high concentration, is also in need of overhauling. Financial difficulties plague most of the remaining State-owned firms and there is, in addition, large scope for exposing the public utilities to greater competition. Correcting these problems requires an overhaul of the regulatory framework, together with more vigorous privatisation initiatives, which should not discriminate against investment by non-residents. Action along these lines would tend to stimulate productivity gains, reducing cost pressures on the export sector and increasing Portuguese competitiveness in general. While the authorities plan to privatise the telecommunications industry, it is important that this be combined with a regulatory framework that leads to the fullest exploitation of the benefits of competition.

Partly reflecting the reforms which have been introduced, Portugal's growth in total factor productivity picked up in the second half of the 1980s, but to an extent which was somewhat disappointing, considering that Portugal has the second lowest per-capita income in the EC. In this context, the strengthening of Portugal's competitive position over the medium term not only requires stronger action to open up the sheltered sector, but also, as noted in previous *Surveys*, continued efforts to upgrade the level of educational attainment and managerial expertise. An important step in this direction has been taken with the new Regional Development Programme, upon which future co-financed investments under the Community Support Framework are to be based. Human capital, infrastructure and the organisational know-how of small and medium-sized enterprises are to be priority areas.

Over the past eighteen months the environment in which stabilisation policies are operating has deteriorated sharply. Continuing statistical deficiencies, which demand prompt and comprehensive remedy, hamper a proper evaluation of the economic situation. However, it is clear that both the large deficit overrun and the two devaluations have reflected a serious shortfall from stated policy objectives. To enhance credibility, it is imperative to make major inroads into the budget deficit, as set out in the new convergence programme. Continued public expenditure restraint is needed for this to be achieved, but strong action is particularly necessary on the revenue side, curbing tax evasion, strengthening tax administration and basing revenue estimates upon more realistic assumptions. Hitting deficit targets would help to convince markets of the authorities' commitment to rebalancing the distorted policy mix, hence offering scope for reducing both inflation expectations and interest rates. Combined with further action to promote structural reform, the prospects for sustained non-inflationary growth would thereby be improved.

Notes and references

1. The decline in car sales may account for up to 1 per cent of the overall slowdown in private consumption. Apart from cyclical conditions, the decline may also reflect the end of a stock-adjustment process started in the second half of the 1980s.

2. An econometric study of wage behaviour in manufacturing over the 1977-1988 period finds that a 1 per cent increase in the unemployment rate reduces nominal wage growth by 1.4 per cent.

3. The coefficient of variation of nominal wage growth across sectors increased by about 8 percentage points in the 1982-1992 period.

4. In 1992 the minimum wage was 48 per cent of the average wage of white and blue-collar workers, down from 50 per cent in 1990; unemployment benefits replaced on average only 41 per cent of earnings per employee, covered only 42 per cent of the registered unemployed and were provided only after eighteen months of contribution.

5. Statistical delays make it difficult to gauge balance-of-trade developments.

6. Banco de Portugal (1993), *Quarterly Bulletin*, Vol. 15, No. 2, June, p. 10.

7. The Bank of Portugal conducts three types of liquidity-absorption operations: regular absorption operations, which are contracted at the beginning of each reserve-maintenance period and which expire on the first business day of the subsequent period; occasional operations of liquidity absorption, which are generally intra-period operations and which are carried out when the overnight money-market rate diverges too strongly from an indicative band; and other operations destined to soak up liquidity. In the case of both regular and occasional liquidity operations, Central Bank monetary certificates are issued. In other transactions, Central Bank intervention bills are sold. See Banco de Portugal (1992), *Quarterly Bulletin*, Vol. 14, No. 4, December, p. 11.

8. For a detailed review see recent OECD *Economic Surveys of Portugal*, 1990/91, 1991/92 and 1993.

9. This limit was not binding in periods of exchange rate turmoil.

10. Under the new facility, banks are allowed to borrow funds at a pre-announced rate at their discretion, subject to a limit for each bank.

11. The consequent rise in domestic liquidity (Esc 2 trillion) would be sterilised through issues of debt instruments by the Bank of Portugal, partly at interest rates below the market level.

12. Indicative lending rate from the Portuguese Banking Association.

13. OECD (1993), *Economic Survey of Portugal*, p. 48.

14. In May 1993, the new central rate was set at Esc 193.0 per ecu as against Esc 182.2 per ecu in November 1992.

15. The targets for nominal primary spending were Esc 3.1 trillion for the state and Esc 5.3 trillion for general government. Only the target for the state sector was binding for the government.

16. The Government estimates that up to 50 per cent of the losses in indirect tax revenues may be explained by this error in evaluating the new tax base.

17. The split between receipts earmarked for debt buyback and restructuring is decided by the government, with no need for parliamentary approval.

18. The medium-term tax gap is defined as the difference between the tax-to-GDP ratio needed to stabilise debt at the 1993 level, given tax and spending policies planned for the next five years, and the actual ratio. See O. Blanchard *et al.* (1990), ''The sustainability of fiscal policy: new answers to an old question'', *OECD Economic Studies*, No. 15, Autumn, pp. 7-36.

19. In 1993, the rating agency Standard and Poor's upgraded Portuguese sovereign debt, long-term and short-term external debt being rated at AA- and A1+, respectively.

20. Transfers to Portugal released under the previous CSF amounted to an annual 3 per cent of GDP, adding 0.7 percentage points to annual real GDP growth over the 1989-93 period. During this period 20 per cent of total investment and 60 per cent of public investment was co-financed by Community funds.

21. Interest earned on housing savings deposits (*Contas Poupança Habitaçao*) will be taxed at a 20 per cent rate, while maximum deductions for other saving plans (*Poupança Emigrante, Planos de Poupança Reforma*) will be lowered.

22. The public employee pension fund (*Caixa Geral de Aposentações*) was incorporated into the state sector in 1993. As a consequence, social contributions and pensions of public employees became part of the revenue and expenditure account of the general government. Pension payments to civil servants will amount to Esc 370 billion in 1994, raising the share of current expenditures in GDP (on a public accounts basis) to 44.5 per cent from 41.9 per cent in 1993.

23. Before the reform, the benefit formula was based on the five best years in the ten-year period prior to retirement and the maximum pension could be obtained after 35 years of contributions. Base salaries are now computed using the ten best years in the fifteen years preceding retirement and 40 years of contribution are needed for obtaining the maximum pension.

24. The reform will apply to all non-residents, including investors in the United States and Japan, which have no double-taxation agreement with Portugal. Investors based in tax havens such as Luxembourg or the Cayman Islands are likely to be excluded.

25. In what follows the non-tradeables sector is equated with the sheltered sector, which is defined as including public and private services as well as construction. Non-tradeables account for 42.5 per cent of the basket for consumer goods and services.

26. S. Rebelo (1993), "Inflation in fixed exchange rate regimes: the recent Portuguese experience", in: *Adjustment and growth in the European Monetary Union*, edited by F. Torres and F. Giavazzi, Cambridge University Press.

27. See W. Baumol (1969), "Macroeconomics of unbalanced growth: The anatomy of urban crisis", *American Economic Review*, pp. 415-26.

28. B. Larre and R. Torres (1991), "Is convergence a spontaneous process? The experience of Spain, Portugal and Greece", *OECD Economic Studies*, No. 16, Spring.

29. A study examining the diffusion of inter-related process innovations in Portugal's clothing industry points to a lack of organisational and managerial know-how as the main factor limiting productivity gains. See M. Godinho (1994): *Innovation Diffusion in the Portuguese and Italian Clothing Industry*, unpublished D. Phil. thesis, Science Policy Research Unit, University of Sussex.

30. At Telecom, one of Portugal's telecommunication companies, productivity growth, as measured by telephone calls per employee, averaged an annual 16 per cent in 1985-91, twice as high as in the previous decade.

31. Banco de Portugal, *op. cit.*, p. 86.

32. See. J. Ferreira Machado and T. Nascimento (1993): "Inflação sectorial", Banco de Portugal, *Quarterly Bulletin*, Vol. 15, No. 3, September.

33. EC (1990), *European Economy: Social Europe*, Special Edition.

34. In addition to import restrictions on clothing, the two most important obstacles to imports have related to levies in processed agricultural products and quantitative restrictions on the manufacture and assembly of motor vehicles (applied up to 1987).

35. OECD (1993), *Economic Outlook*, 54, p. 35.

36. Petrogal was partly privatised in July 1992, when the government sold 25 per cent of the equity to private shareholders, subject to the provision that foreign investors cannot directly or indirectly hold a majority of the company's privately-owned capital. Private shareholders were grouped together in the holding company Petrocontrol. Under the privatisation terms applicable to Petrogal, Petrocontrol could have bought an additional 26 per cent of the equity by March 1993. The option was not used and expires in July 1995, when a penalty clause requires Petrocontrol to forfeit 6 per cent of the 25 per cent it already owns. The complete sale of Petrogal is made more difficult by its financial problems: net losses in 1993 totalled Esc 16 billion as debt servicing costs outweighed an operating profit, and at 4.2 the debt to equity ratio far exceeded that of other European oil companies.

37. A law, permitting partial privatisation, had already been adopted in 1988, enabling public enterprises to be transformed into corporations, with the State retaining 51 per cent of total equity. Four firms (a bank, two insurance companies and one brewery) were partially privatised prior to June 1989 using two different laws (No. 74 and No. 84).

38. In 1992 alone, a total of 14 companies were partly or fully privatised, yielding proceeds worth 2.7 per cent of GDP.

39. Compensation paid to previous owners began only to be made in the early 1980s, based upon provisional valuation, not subject to appeal. Shareholders received long-term government bonds, carrying a fixed interest rate well below the rate of inflation. A final assessment of the

companies' value was to be made by independent tribunals. When privatisations started, in some cases no payments had been made.

40. Government intervention need not produce rent-seeking behaviour. Shielded against interference from pressure groups, regulatory agencies may apply ''contest-based incentives'' and continuous monitoring to prevent this. See The World Bank (1993), *The East Asian Miracle*, Oxford University Press.

41. There is some evidence that natural monopoly conditions prevailed in Portugal's telecommunication services at the end of the 1970s. Granting access to more producers of telephone services could then have raised the industry's total costs. See M. do Carmen Seabra (1993), ''Natural monopoly in Portuguese telecommunications'', *Applied Economics*, Vol. 25, pp. 489-494.

42. TLP handles more than half of the country's telephone traffic. Covering an area holding 37 per cent of the population, roughly half of Portugal's purchasing power and 80 per cent of corporate headquarters, TLP is one of Portugal's top business corporations, ranking fourth in terms of value added and net assets.

43. Starting from only 19 phones per 100 inhabitants in 1985, Portugal had a density of about 30 by the end of 1992 compared with 44 for Europe as a whole. In urban centres, Portugal has almost reached the European average.

44. Starting in 1993, this airline also flies on the Lisbon-Porto route, of which it has a 46 per cent market share.

45. H. Gibson and E. Tsakalotos (1993), ''European integration and the banking sector in Southern Europe: competition, efficiency and structure'', *Banca Nazionale del Lavoro Quarterly Review*, No. 186.

46. The crucial role which foreign direct investment plays in raising efficiency has been confirmed by a recent study, showing it to have been more important than trade in the United States and Germany. See Mc Kinsey Global Institute (1993), *Manufacturing Productivity*.

47. See OECD (1994), *Portugal: Examination of foreign direct investment measures under the code of liberalisation of capital movements and the national treatment instrument*.

48. See OECD (1991), *Economic Survey of Portugal*, pp. 32-36; OECD (1992), *Economic Survey of Portugal*, pp. 56-66; and OECD (1993), *Economic Survey of Portugal*, pp. 45-48.

49. In March 1989, the Bank of Portugal imposed a common reserve coefficient of 17 per cent on all deposits and raised the remuneration of bank reserves. In May 1990, the reserve requirement was broadened to cover a wider range of short-term assets, including repurchase agreements.

50. By 1993, most banks had solvency ratios in excess of 8 per cent, the level required by the EC's Second Banking Directive.

51. From 1990 to 1992, foreign banks wishing to buy stakes in State-owned banks or to establish branches in Portugal had to make a payment of about Esc 900 million, or nearly US$7 million. Payments went to Finnagest, a state-owned institution dealing with bad loans of State-owned banks. See Gibson and Tsakalotos, *op. cit.*, p. 313.

52. At the end of 1992, there was one branch for every 3 300 people, compared with a ratio of around 5 000 in the EC.

53. In 1991, the group *Banco Português de Investimento*, the largest Portuguese investment bank, purchased the state-owned *Banco Fonsecas & Burnay*.

54. The stamp tax is levied at a rate of 9 per cent of interest payments. The reserve coefficient of 17 per cent also implied a high ''tax'' on deposits as long as reserves were unremunerated. However, such deposits have yielded market rate returns since the end of January 1991.

55. See M. Catalão Lopes (1992), ''Estimação do poder de mercado no mercado de crédito português'', Banco do Portugal, *Quarterly Bulletin*, Vol. 14, No. 4, December.

56. Commission of the European Communities (1993), *The economic and financial situation in Italy*, No. 1, pp. 165-168.

57. A further cause may be Portugal's death rate from motor accidents, which was the highest in the world in 1991, leading to high insurance premia. *The Economist*, 20 November 1993.

58. Commission of the European Communities, *op. cit.* p. 167.

59. See Center for European Policy Studies (1993), ''Financing retirement in Europe'', *CEPS Working Party Report No. 9*.

60. For food sales, the market share of traditional shops is 74 per cent.

61. The authorisation for opening a new large retail or wholesale outlet depends upon a study analysing its potential impact on the local economy.

62. A few goods and services are still subject to controls. For some (*e.g.* , water, electricity, gas, mandatory school textbooks, and taxis) prices are set by consultation with producers; for others, in particular therapeutic drugs, a cost-plus rule is followed. On the other hand, contrary to most OECD countries, book prices cannot be fixed by publishers.

63. Article 5.1 states that ''restrictive practices on competition which contribute to improvements in the production or distribution of goods or services or promote technical or economic development may be considered justified if: *a)* they reserve for users of those goods or services a fair share of the resulting benefits; *b)* they do not impose on the undertakings in question any restrictions which are not essential for the attainment of these objectives; *c)* they do not provide the undertakings in question with the opportunity to eliminate the competition in a substantial part of the market in the goods and services in question''.

64. For a discussion of these issues, see OECD (1994), *Economic Survey of Italy*, p. 120-121.

65. A new proposition, ''efficient component pricing'' (ECP), put forward by Baumol and Sidak, rehabilitates the principle of marginal cost pricing for setting access fees. Network owners, who are also in the market for final products, will lose revenues to any newcomer. According to Baumol and Sidak, this ''opportunity cost'' should be included in the access fee. All told, ECP has three major advantages: it sends the right signals to new suppliers; network costs are covered; and there is no need to separate the network from the supply of final products. Faced with the right access price, incumbents have no incentive to keep rivals out. On the other hand, ECP may not ensure the erosion of monopoly profits, calling for continued regulation. W. Baumol and G. Sidak, *Toward competition in local telephony*, MIT Press and the American Enterprise Institute, 1994; A. Kahn (1993), ''Opening up utilities'', letter addressed to *The Economist*, December 25.

66. This option has been introduced in Britain's electricity industry.

Annex I

Supporting material to Part III

Table A.1. The "sheltered" sector

Output shares	1980	1986	1990
	In per cent of GDP at 1985 prices		
Construction	6.4	5.6	5.8
Wholesale and retail trade	21.0	19.1	19.0
Restaurants and hotels	3.3	3.4	3.7
Transport, storage, communication	6.8	7.7	8.5
Financial institutions	5.4	5.5	8.3
Insurance	0.6	0.5	0.3
Real estate and business services	4.0	3.9	4.4
Community, social and personal services	3.0	3.1	2.8
Producers of government services	11.1	12.4	11.3
Total	61.6	61.2	61.1
Employment shares	In per cent of total employment		
Construction	10.1	8.9	9.9
Wholesale and retail trade	10.6	10.9	13.2
Restaurants and hotels	2.8	3.6	3.9
Transport, storage, communication	4.5	4.5	4.4
Financial institutions	1.3	1.6	1.6
Insurance	0.3	0.4	0.4
Real estate and business services	0.9	1.0	1.1
Community, social and personal services	1.9	2.5	2.5
Producers of government services	10.0	12.8	13.6
Total	42.4	46.2	50.6

Source: OECD, *National Accounts.*

88

Diagram A1. **GDP PER CAPITA AND RELATIVE PRICE LEVELS**
Using PPPs, OECD = 100

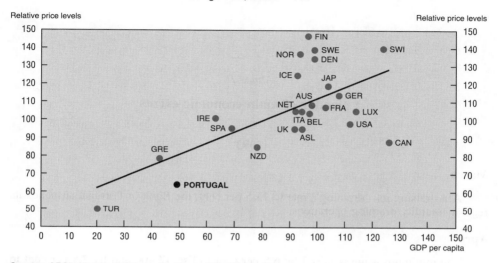

Relative price levels

Relative price levels

GDP per capita

Source: OECD, *Purchasing Power Parities and Real Expenditures.*

Calendar of main economic events

1993

March

After raising its "draining" rate to 13.5 per cent, the Bank of Portugal suspends its regular liquidity draining operations.

April

The minimum wage is raised by 6.5 per cent to Esc 47 400 and by 7.5 per cent to Esc 41 000 for household services.

New measures are announced to stimulate the economy, increasing public spending on infrastructures (housing, EXPO 98 in Lisbon) and assisting exporting companies.

May

The Bank of Portugal resumes its draining operations, suspended in March, lifting the intervention rate to 17 per cent.

The central rate of the escudo against other currencies of the ERM is adjusted downwards by 6.5 per cent.

The central bank's "draining" rate is lowered in two stages to 12 per cent.

Portugal's external long-term debt is awarded a AA mark by Standard & Poor, while the internal one is awarded a triple A.

June

The Bank of Portugal reduces its "draining" rate in three stages to 10.5 per cent.

July

Remuneration of minimum cash reserves is reduced to 9.875 per cent from 12.875 per cent.

After lowering its "draining" rate to 10.25 per cent, the Bank of Portugal suspends regular intervention on the domestic money market. The rate applicable to the daily facility is set at 14.5 per cent.

August

The rate applicable to the daily facility is reduced in four steps to 12.375 per cent.

September

The rate applicable to the daily facility is reduced to 12.250 per cent.

October

The rate applicable to the daily facility is reduced in two stages to 12.0 per cent.

The Bank of Portugal resumes its regular intervention on the domestic money market, setting the "draining" rate at 10.375 per cent and the "injection" rate at 11.375 per cent.

November

The supplementary budget for 1993 is approved.

The Bank of Portugal reduces its "draining" rate to 10.250 per cent and the "injection" rate to 11.250 per cent.

December

The Bank of Portugal reduces in two stages the "draining" rate to 10.0 per cent and the "injection" rate to 11.0 per cent.

1994

January

The Bank of Portugal lowers in three steps its "draining" rate to 9.5 per cent and the "injection" rate to 10.5 per cent. The rate applicable to the daily facility is reduced to 11.5 per cent.

February

The Bank of Portugal reduces its "draining" rate to 9.25 per cent and the "injection" rate to 10.25 per cent.

EU Ministers approve the Country Support Framework (CSF), governing the flow of EU transfers to Portugal over the next five years.

STATISTICAL AND STRUCTURAL ANNEX

Selected background statistics

	Average 1983-92	1983	1984	1985	1986	1987	1988	1989	1990	1991	1992
A. Percentage changes											
Private consumption[1]	3.2	-1.4	-2.9	0.7	5.6	5.4	6.6	3.3	5.3	5.2	4.4
Government consumption[1]	3.6	3.8	0.2	6.4	7.2	4.9	5.3	2.8	1.5	3.0	1.4
Gross fixed capital formation[1]	2.8	-7.1	-17.4	-3.5	10.9	15.1	15.0	5.6	5.9	2.4	5.7
Total domestic demand[1]	3.1	-5.7	-6.7	0.9	8.3	10.4	7.4	4.3	5.4	4.1	4.1
Exports of goods and services[1]	8.8	13.6	11.6	6.7	6.8	8.6	10.2	13.3	9.5	1.1	6.8
Imports of goods and services[1]	7.4	-6.1	-4.4	1.4	16.9	20.0	16.1	9.1	10.1	4.9	9.7
GDP[1]	2.7	-0.2	-1.9	2.8	4.1	5.3	3.9	5.2	4.4	2.1	1.6
GDP price deflator	16.9	24.6	24.6	21.8	20.4	11.2	11.6	13.0	14.3	14.1	14.0
Industrial production	3.5	3.6	2.3	0.9	7.3	4.3	3.6	7.0	9.2	0	-3.0
Employment	0.9	3.9	-0.1	-0.5	0.2	2.6	2.6	2.2	2.2	3.0	-6.4
Compensation of employees (current prices)	18.4	21.8	18.2	20.7	20.0	18.8	14.5	15.3	21.0	19.2	15.0
Productivity (real GDP/employment)	1.8	-4.0	-1.8	3.3	3.9	2.6	1.3	2.9	2.1	-0.8	8.6
Unit labour costs (compensation/real GDP)	15.3	22.1	20.5	17.4	15.2	12.9	10.2	9.7	15.9	16.7	13.1
B. Percentage ratios											
Gross fixed capital formation as per cent of GDP at constant prices	26.5	27.6	23.2	21.8	23.2	25.4	28.1	28.2	28.6	28.7	29.8
Stockbuilding as per cent of GDP at constant prices	1.5	-0.9	-1.6	-1.2	0.2	3.2	2.4	2.9	3.4	3.4	3.2
Foreign balance as per cent of GDP at constant prices	-13.6	-11.5	-6.0	-4.1	-8.2	-13.5	-17.3	-16.3	-17.4	-19.7	-22.6
Compensation of employees as per cent of GDP at current prices	46.5	51.0	49.3	47.5	45.5	46.1	45.6	44.2	44.9	45.9	45.6
Direct taxes as per cent of household income	5.9	6.1	5.7	6.1	5.3	4.0	5.2	6.5	5.9	6.9	7.5
Household saving as per cent of disposable income	24.8	26.7	27.7	28.7	26.3	25.6	22.3	22.4	23.3	23.0	22.2
Unemployment rate[2]	6.5	7.8	8.5	8.7	8.6	7.2	5.8	5.1	4.7	4.1	4.2
C. Other indicator											
Current balance (billion dollars)	-0.2	-1.5	-0.6	0.3	1.2	0.4	-1.0	0.2	-0.2	-0.7	-0.2

1. At constant 1985 prices.
2. Data based on the narrowest definition of unemployment.
Sources: National Institute of Statistics (INE); Bank of Portugal; OECD estimates.

Table A. **Expenditure on gross domestic product**

Billion escudos

	1982	1983	1984	1985	1986	1987	1988	1989	1990	1991	1992
A. At current prices											
Private consumption	1 287.1	1 596.2	1 990.3	2 393.2	2 876.2	3 335.7	3 909.9	4 527.1	5 368.7	6 273.8	7 143.8
Government consumption	276.2	348.4	423.1	546.9	678.8	787.8	962.2	1 147.4	1 422.8	1 765.9	2 077.2
Gross fixed investment	574.8	671.5	663.7	768.0	977.0	1 250.8	1 611.2	1 885.0	2 243.3	2 574.9	2 982.0
Stockbuilding	56.4	–20.8	–37.7	–40.8	10.6	171.0	169.8	192.2	231.2	231.2	266.1
Total domestic demand	2 194.4	2 595.2	3 039.4	3 667.3	4 542.6	5 545.3	6 653.1	7 751.7	9 266.1	10 845.8	12 469.1
Exports	488.5	721.2	1 048.6	1 315.2	1 466.6	1 774.7	2 129.5	2 671.1	3 100.2	3 166.3	3 302.1
Imports	832.5	1 014.8	1 272.3	1 458.6	1 588.8	2 145.2	2 779.9	3 292.6	3 858.8	4 098.7	4 405.2
GDP (at market prices)	1 850.4	2 301.7	2 815.7	3 523.9	4 420.4	5 174.7	6 002.8	7 130.3	8 507.4	9 913.4	11 366.0
B. At 1985 prices											
Private consumption	2 484.9	2 449.3	2 377.2	2 393.2	2 527.0	2 663.1	2 838.3	2 932.1	3 088.0	3 248.2	3 369.6
Government consumption	494.0	512.7	513.9	546.9	586.1	614.6	647.2	665.0	674.7	694.9	704.7
Gross fixed investment	1 037.8	963.8	796.2	768.0	851.4	979.7	1 126.3	1 189.8	1 260.4	1 291.2	1 361.4
Stockbuilding	114.2	–31.7	–54.2	–40.8	6.1	125.3	96.0	121.7	150.8	151.3	202.3
Total domestic demand	4 130.9	3 894.1	3 633.0	3 667.3	3 970.7	4 382.7	4 707.9	4 908.6	5 173.9	5 385.6	5 638.0
Exports	972.2	1 104.5	1 233.0	1 315.2	1 404.1	1 525.0	1 680.2	1 903.4	2 084.1	2 107.8	2 236.7
Imports	1 603.7	1 505.2	1 438.3	1 458.6	1 704.8	2 045.1	2 374.0	2 591.0	2 852.4	2 993.3	3 325.9
GDP (at market prices)	3 499.4	3 493.4	3 427.7	3 523.9	3 669.9	3 862.6	4 014.1	4 221.0	4 405.6	4 500.1	4 548.8

Sources: National Institute of Statistics (INE); Bank of Portugal.

Table B. **Household appropriation account**

Billion escudos

	1983	1984	1985	1986	1987	1988	1989	1990	1991	1992
Compensation of employees	1 173.3	1 386.8	1 674.0	2 008.9	2 386.6	2 733.8	3 153.4	3 816.2	4 550.5	5 233.1
Property and entrepreneurial income	923.6	1 229.9	1 552.4	1 686.5	1 795.9	2 047.4	2 504.2	2 956.8	3 429.8	3 892.9
Domestic transfers	294.6	361.3	440.1	595.9	763.6	881.3	1 021.6	1 242.6	1 523.9	1 828.3
Foreign transfers	242.0	320.3	358.3	395.6	479.9	520.6	587.9	637.9	695.3	757.9
Gross total income	2 633.5	3 298.3	4 024.8	4 686.9	5 426.0	6 183.1	7 267.1	8 653.5	10 199.5	11 712.2
Direct taxes	161.3	188.6	244.8	249.0	218.1	324.0	468.9	512.2	704.1	878.5
Social security contributions	305.1	372.0	440.5	555.1	746.2	850.9	989.5	1 179.0	1 388.2	1 620.6
Disposable income	2 167.1	2 737.7	3 339.5	3 882.7	4 461.7	5 008.1	5 808.7	6 962.3	8 107.3	9 213.1
Consumption	1 587.6	1 980.4	2 381.4	2 861.8	3 320.0	3 891.6	4 506.0	5 343.0	6 244.9	7 163.9
Real disposable income, percentage change	-3.7	-1.6	2.1	2.2	4.4	2.1	3.5	6.5	4.8	3.9

1. As a percentage of disposable income.
Sources: Ministry of Finance; Bank of Portugal.

Table C. General government account

Billion escudos

	1983	1984	1985	1986	1987	1988	1989	1990	1991	1992
Current receipts	869.2	1 051.1	1 266.7	1 660.2	1 873.2	2 285.6	2 756.1	3 196.4	4 322.2	5 399.5
Direct taxes	206.7	246.7	313.3	322.0	319.4	463.3	668.0	764.6	1 005.8	1 255.0
Social security contributions	244.6	298.5	354.0	449.2	602.1	691.3	797.0	949.8	1 119.5	1 306.9
Indirect taxes	358.5	436.8	534.2	767.9	804.8	1 002.8	1 104.5	1 308.8	1 453.6	1 777.9
Capital income	47.7	54.2	46.2	76.9	95.4	83.2	114.8	137.1	268.3	430.4
Other current receipts	11.8	14.9	19.1	44.2	51.4	45.1	71.8	36.1	475.0	629.3
Current expenditure	835.4	1 085.0	1 389.5	1 787.4	2 023.9	2 342.0	2 683.7	3 347.4	4 263.8	5 084.9
Expenditure on goods and services	348.4	423.1	546.9	678.8	787.8	962.2	1 147.4	1 422.8	1 742.4	2 063.6
Subsidies	91.8	120.1	127.1	131.1	98.4	109.5	105.5	106.5	153.9	158.1
Interest paid	141.4	231.0	329.0	428.1	453.0	467.6	507.4	692.3	832.2	1 020.5
Current transfers	209.6	255.3	315.5	402.9	486.2	582.0	665.2	804.8	1 177.4	1 372.1
Saving	33.9	-33.8	-122.8	-127.2	-150.7	-56.4	72.5	-151.0	58.4	314.6
Capital expenditure	266.7	163.1	137.2	151.9	224.4	267.9	287.7	299.0	653.0	838.9
Fixed investment	88.6	90.7	108.9	144.0	170.9	216.9	246.1	290.9	376.6	481.5
Transfers	178.1	72.4	28.3	8.0	53.5	50.9	41.6	8.1	276.4	357.4
Overall balance	-233.1	-198.4	-261.3	-281.5	-377.9	-326.8	-218.3	-453.9	-599.5	-530.6
(as a percentage of GDP)	-10.1	-7.0	-7.4	-6.4	-7.3	-5.4	-3.1	-5.3	-6.0	-4.6
Loans	30.9	39.3	37.1	78.0	107.5	82.2	97.9	84.4	46.9	31.9
Total borrowing requirement	-264.0	-237.7	-298.4	-359.5	-485.4	-409.0	-316.2	-538.3	-646.4	-562.5
(as a percentage of GDP)	-11.5	-8.4	-8.5	-8.1	-9.4	-6.8	-4.4	-6.3	-6.5	-4.9

Source: Ministry of Finance.

Table D. **Prices and wages**

	1983	1984	1985	1986	1987	1988	1989	1990	1991	1992
Percentage changes										
Consumer prices[1]										
Total[2]	25.5	29.3	19.3	11.7	9.4	9.6	12.6	13.4	11.4	8.9
Food and drink	25.1	30.8	17.7	9.1	8.8	9.2	14.4	13.6	9.9	7.1
Clothing and footwear	19.8	24.4	23.3	23.5	15.8	13.2	10.5	9.5	11.9	11.9
Housing costs	29.0	33.8	20.0	10.7	7.4	10.1	11.8	11.9	12.1	9.6
Miscellaneous	27.8	24.7	21.9	14.5	9.0	6.0	11.6	11.3	10.9	8.6
Wages in manufacturing industry										
Nominal	18.7	18.8	21.1	16.8	14.0	11.3	14.8	16.2	16.3	14.7
Real	–5.4	–7.8	1.2	4.5	4.2	1.5	2.0	2.5	4.4	5.3

1. Mainland. New index as from 1988.
2. Excluding rent.
Sources: INE; Bank of Portugal; OECD, *Main Economic Indicators.*

98

Table E. Civilian employment by sector

Thousands

	1983	1984	1985	1986	1987	1988	1989	1990	1991	1992
Agriculture	933.9	931.1	933.0	891.0	926.0	885.0	829.0	796.3	804.0	563.0
Mining	28.3	28.2	28.3	27.0	27.0	29.0	20.0	34.1	23.0	23.0
Manufacturing	1 040.8	1 029.4	1 010.8	995.0	1 040.0	1 074.0	1 107.0	1 082.5	1 129.0	1 094.0
Construction	298.8	305.7	328.3	332.0	354.0	362.0	384.0	351.9	367.0	366.0
Electricity, gas and water	44.4	39.7	34.8	32.0	33.0	38.0	38.0	38.1	42.0	32.0
Transport and communication	190.2	187.5	179.8	174.0	168.0	177.0	180.0	183.2	223.0	220.0
Trade	659.7	638.6	610.5	599.0	585.0	630.0	655.0	663.7	744.0	907.0
Banking, insurance, real estate	134.7	135.0	131.9	127.0	132.0	140.0	154.0	162.3	214.0	298.0
Personal services	883.5	889.7	885.2	887.0	906.0	945.0	1 009.0	1 008.0	1 097.0	1 122.0
Total	4 214.3	4 184.9	4 142.6	4 064.0	4 171.0	4 280.0	4 376.0	4 320.1	4 643.0	4 625.0

Sources: OECD, *Labour Force Statistics* and OECD estimates.

Table F. **Money supply and its counterparts**

Billion escudos at end of period

	1983	1984	1985	1986	1987	1988	1989	1990	1991	1992
Total money supply (L)	2 650	3 386	4 311	5 280	6 045	6 893	7 553	8 883	10 644	12 370
Money (M1−)										
Notes and coins in circulation	666	772	981	1 334	1 527	1 722	1 828	2 352	2 705	3 164
Sight deposits of households and enterprises	240	267	319	399	458	510	577	624	683	708
	426	505	662	935	1 069	1 213	1 251	1 728	2 022	2 456
Quasi money[1]	1 984	2 613	3 330	3 946	4 519	5 171	5 725	6 531	7 939	9 206
Counterparts										
Net foreign assets	566	774	973	935	1 181	1 827	2 512	2 716	3 447	3 753
Net lending to the public sector	654	901	1 349	1 866	2 332	2 616	2 546	2 797	2 823	3 136
Lending to the private sector	2 103	2 546	2 785	3 097	3 200	3 526	3 704	4 982	6 284	7 503
Miscellaneous, net	−672	−834	−796	−618	−667	−1 076	−1 209	−1 611	−1 910	−2 022

1. Including migrant deposits and Treasury bills.
Source: Bank of Portugal, *Quarterly Bulletin.*

Table G. **Breakdown by nationality of foreign visitors**

Thousands

	1983	1984	1985	1986	1987	1988	1989	1990	1991	1992
Total	8 875	9 811	11 692	13 057	16 173	16 077	16 471	18 422	19 641	20 742
Spain	6 513	7 309	8 798	9 960	12 583	12 124	12 186	13 806	14 583	15 553
United Kingdom	630	710	880	1 069	1 204	1 140	1 137	1 203	1 307	1 435
Germany	355	344	413	430	526	569	611	681	852	877
France	328	327	347	350	435	593	646	658	712	686
Netherlands	156	152	164	172	214	285	333	330	361	367
United States	187	209	230	150	195	223	235	252	178	220
Italy	66	72	93	109	134	155	185	221	291	283
Brazil	57	60	69	83	72	92	102	119	114	106
Canada	47	56	70	74	78	79	91	91	69	74
Sweden	66	72	54	69	70	87	95	98	114	108
Belgium	61	59	68	68	90	117	151	173	198	207
Switzerland	46	53	61	66	71	73	78	78	80	73
Other countries	363	389	444	457	502	540	621	713	782	752

Source: INE, *Boletim mensal de estatística.*

Table H. Foreign trade by main commodity groups
Million US dollars and percentages

	1983	1984	1985	1986	1987	1988	1989	1990	1991	1992
Imports, total (million $)	8 256.7	7 975.3	7 649.7	9 454.0	13 965.7	17 884.8	19 043.1	25 332.6	26 328.6	30 482.4
As a percentage of total										
Food and beverages	10.7	11.5	11.0	11.0	10.6	10.3	9.9	9.7	11.2	11.1
Basic material and semi-finished goods	37.1	42.3	39.1	25.0	19.4	15.9	17.5	16.9	14.5	12.6
Manufactures	51.9	46.0	49.6	63.4	69.6	73.7	72.5	73.3	74.2	76.3
Chemicals	10.0	9.9	10.2	11.3	10.5	9.8	9.2	9.1	9.0	9.0
Goods classified chiefly by material	12.4	12.0	14.5	17.7	19.2	19.2	19.8	19.6	19.5	19.1
Machinery and transport equipment	26.1	21.1	21.6	29.3	33.9	38.3	36.8	36.9	36.5	38.2
Miscellaneous	3.4	3.0	3.3	5.1	6.1	6.3	6.7	7.7	9.2	10.0
Unspecified	0.3	0.2	0.3	0.6	0.3	0.1	0.1	0.1	0.1	0.1
Exports, total (million $)	4 601.4	5 207.5	5 685.4	7 204.9	9 318.3	10 989.7	12 797.7	16 415.7	16 326.1	18 540.6
As a percentage of total										
Food and beverages	9.6	8.8	7.8	8.2	7.3	7.7	7.0	6.6	7.3	7.0
Basic material and semi-finished goods	15.6	15.2	14.5	12.2	11.9	12.8	14.0	12.8	10.5	9.9
Manufactures	72.6	75.3	76.0	78.4	80.1	79.1	78.6	80.3	81.9	82.9
Chemicals	7.5	7.7	7.0	6.1	5.4	6.0	5.6	5.2	4.6	4.2
Goods classified chiefly by material	28.7	28.1	27.7	26.4	25.4	25.4	23.7	23.4	24.1	23.4
Machinery and transport equipment	15.4	17.3	15.6	15.7	16.5	16.7	19.1	19.6	19.7	21.6
Miscellaneous	21.0	22.2	25.7	30.3	32.8	31.0	30.3	32.1	33.6	33.6
Unspecified	2.2	0.8	1.7	1.2	0.7	0.4	0.4	0.3	0.3	0.2

Source: OECD, Foreign Trade Statistics, Series C.

Table I. **Geographical breakdown of foreign trade**
Billion escudos and percentages

	1983	1984	1985	1986	1987	1988	1989	1990	1991	1992
Exports, total	536.8	795.7	950.4	1 055.0	1 304.1	1 598.1	2 035.5	2 255.6	2 405.2	2 436.8
As a percentage of total										
OECD countries	82.8	84.1	85.4	89.1	91.0	90.6	90.7	91.2	90.9	89.1
EC	63.1	62.1	62.6	68.3	71.1	72.0	71.8	73.9	75.4	74.5
Germany	13.6	13.8	13.8	14.7	15.4	14.7	15.7	16.7	19.1	19.0
France	13.7	12.5	12.7	15.2	15.8	15.2	15.0	15.5	14.4	14.0
Italy	4.1	4.3	4.0	3.9	3.9	4.2	4.3	4.1	4.0	3.8
United Kingdom	14.7	15.4	14.6	14.2	14.1	14.3	12.3	12.1	10.8	11.1
Spain	4.1	4.4	4.2	6.9	9.3	11.5	12.7	13.5	15.1	14.7
Other EC	13.0	11.7	13.4	13.3	12.6	12.1	11.8	11.9	12.0	11.8
United States	6.0	8.8	9.2	7.0	6.4	5.9	5.9	4.8	3.8	3.5
Other OECD countries	13.7	13.1	13.6	13.8	13.5	12.6	12.9	12.5	11.8	11.1
Non OECD countries	15.5	14.5	13.3	10.0	8.2	8.1	8.3	7.8	8.1	10.0
of which: OPEC	3.6	2.5	2.5	1.6	1.5	1.1	0.7	0.6	0.5	0.6
Previous Escudo Area	4.5	4.4	3.9	2.1	2.1	2.7	3.3	3.4	4.2	5.4
Imports, total	947.1	1 193.7	1 281.3	1 399.4	1 955.1	2 596.7	3 033.4	3 467.6	3 893.7	4 015.7
As a percentage of total										
OECD countries	69.8	66.7	67.1	78.4	81.7	84.0	83.5	83.4	85.4	86.7
EC	44.9	43.3	46.1	58.9	63.8	67.3	68.2	69.2	72.0	73.3
Germany	11.5	10.2	11.7	14.4	15.1	14.7	14.6	14.4	15.0	14.9
France	8.1	7.9	8.0	10.0	11.2	11.5	11.7	11.5	11.9	12.7
Italy	5.1	4.7	5.1	7.9	8.7	9.3	9.1	10.0	10.2	10.2
United Kingdom	7.7	6.8	7.5	7.5	8.1	8.3	7.5	7.6	7.5	7.1
Spain	5.2	7.1	7.4	11.0	11.7	13.2	14.5	14.4	15.8	16.5
Other EC	7.3	6.4	6.3	8.2	8.9	10.3	10.8	11.3	11.5	11.9
United States	14.3	13.6	9.7	7.0	4.8	4.3	4.4	3.9	3.4	3.1
Other OECD countries	10.6	9.8	11.3	12.4	13.0	12.5	10.8	10.3	10.1	10.3
Non OECD countries	29.7	32.8	32.0	21.2	18.2	15.9	16.5	16.6	14.5	13.3
of which: OPEC	18.6	18.9	17.6	8.5	6.0	4.9	6.1	6.7	4.7	3.9
Previous Escudo Area	0.4	0.7	1.2	0.8	0.4	0.2	0.4	0.4	0.5	0.5

Source: INE, *Boletim mensal das estatísticas do comercio externo.*

Table J. **Balance of payments**

Million US dollars

	1983	1984	1985	1986	1987	1988	1989	1990	1991	1992
Exports, fob	4 569	5 177	5 673	7 202	9 268	10 875	12 716	16 301	16 223	18 275
Imports, fob	7 643	7 307	7 177	8 882	12 849	16 393	17 594	23 129	24 078	27 675
Trade balance	-3 074	-2 130	-1 504	-1 680	-3 581	-5 518	-4 878	-6 828	-7 855	-9 400
Services, net	-742	-674	-361	-85	250	137	478	1 147	1 151	1 583
Travel	588	728	901	1 203	1 721	1 869	2 102	2 688	2 686	2 556
Transports	-200	-192	-184	-135	-373	-587	-663	-889	-1 023	-1 104
Investment income	-1 066	-1 202	-1 152	-1 014	-932	-877	-718	-233	82	666
Government transactions	-37	-40	-44	-56	-123	-131	-135	-162	-182	-189
Other services	-27	32	118	-83	-43	-137	-108	-257	-412	-346
Transfers, net	2 171	2 179	2 251	2 915	3 775	4 317	4 539	5 500	5 962	7 797
Current balance	-1 645	-625	386	1 150	444	-1 064	139	-181	-742	-20
Medium and long-term capital	1 458	1 333	1 109	-293	194	843	2 798	3 576	3 981	-612
Private	858	835	729	-196	195	811	2 243	2 215	2 936	-695
Official	600	498	380	-97	-1	32	555	1 361	1 045	83
Short-term and unrecorded	-564	-221	-523	-1 079	1 273	1 826	993	553	1 766	983
Non-monetary transactions, net	-751	487	972	-222	1 911	1 605	3 930	3 948	5 005	351
Private monetary institutions short-term capital	-310	-289	4	199	-101	-671	633	-446	771	-550
Balance on official settlements	-1 061	198	976	-23	1 810	934	4 563	3 502	5 776	-199
Use of IMF credit	366	221	0	0	0	0	0	0	0	0
Miscellaneous official accounts	0	-287	-284	-82	-309	-556	92	26	-87	10
Changes in reserves (increase = -)	695	-132	-692	105	-1 501	-378	-4 655	-3 528	-5 689	189

Source: Bank of Portugal.

Table K. **Labour-market indicators**

A. LABOUR MARKET PERFORMANCE

	Cyclical Peak: 1979	Cyclical Trough: 1984	1985	1992
Standardised unemployment rate	. .	8.4	8.5	4.1
Unemployment rate: Total	7.5	8.1	8.1	4.1
Male	4.0	5.7	6.1	3.5
Women	12.5	11.3	11.0	4.9
Youth[2]	17.8	19.6	19.5	10.0
Share of long-term unemployment in total unemployment[3]	. .	47.0	52.9	26.8

B. STRUCTURAL OR INSTITUTIONAL CHARACTERISTICS

	1975	1980	1985	1992[1]
Participation rate[4]: Total	70.7	71.8	71.8	70.7
Male	93.3	90.8	85.8	81.4
Women	50.6	54.9	58.8	60.9
Employment/population (15-64 years)	66.4	65.0	64.5	67.8
Non-wage labour costs[5] (as a percentage of total compensation)	13.4	13.8	19.8	19.1
Unemployment insurance replacement ratio[6]	. .	32.4	28.8	26.5
Minimum wage, non-agricultural sector (workers of 20 years and more, as a percentage of the average earnings)	. .	. .	. .	48.2

Average percentage changes (annual rates)	1970 / 1960	1980 / 1970	1985 / 1980	1992 / 1986
Labour force	0.5	2.0	0.7	0.9
Employment: Total	0.4	1.4	0.5	1.7
Industries	0.7	2.7	−0.9	0.8
Services	4.3	1.4	3.8	6.9

1. Long-term unemployment, employment/population, unemployment insurance : 1989.
2. People between 15 and 24 years as a percentage of the labour force of the same age group.
3. Persons seeking a job for 12 months and over as a percentage of total unemployed.
4. Labour force as a percentage of relevant population group, aged between 15 and 64 years.
5. Employers' contributions to social security and pension funds.
6. Unemployment benefits per unemployed as a percentage of compensation per employee.
Sources: OECD, *Labour Force Statistics;* OECD Secretariat.

Table L. **Public sector**

A. BUDGET INDICATORS : GENERAL GOVERNMENT ACCOUNT
Per cent of GDP[1]

	1970	1980	1985	1992
Current receipts	25.6	31.4	35.9	44.1
Non-interest expenditure	22.8	36.4	36.8	43.6
Primary budget balance	3.3	−4.8	−0.4	4.3
Interest payments	0.5	3.1	8.1	9.1
General government budget balance	2.8	−7.9	−8.5	−4.7

B. THE STRUCTURE OF GENERAL GOVERNMENT EXPENDITURE
Per cent of GDP

	1970	1980	1985	1992
Total expenditure	23.4	39.5	44.8	52.6
of which: Current consumption	14.0	14.5	14.3	18.3
Transfers to persons	4.0	10.7	12.8	15.5
Subsidies	1.5	5.2	4.1	1.4
Capital formation	2.5	4.1	3.1	4.3

1. On a national accounts basis.
Sources: OECD, *National Accounts; Revenue Statistics of OECD Member Countries.*

Table M. **Production and employment structures**

	Per cent share of GDP at factor cost (current prices)				Per cent share of total employment			
	1977	1980	1985	1990	1977	1980	1985	1990
Agriculture, forestry and fishing	11.9	10.3	8.0	5.8	31.8	27.2	25.4	20.3
Manufacturing	27.9	31.0	30.4	27.9	23.6	25.1	24.3	23.8
of which: Food, forestry and tobacco	5.7	5.7	6.1	6.0	3.5	3.3	3.2	3.3
Textiles, clothing, leather	5.4	7.0	7.8	7.2	7.6	8.1	8.3	8.3
Wood, paper and paper products	3.4	3.7	3.2	3.1	3.1	3.2	2.9	2.7
Chemicals and products of petroleum, coal, rubber, etc.	3.0	2.8	3.3	2.1	1.5	1.7	1.6	1.5
Non-mineral products except products of petroleum and coal	2.4	2.6	2.1	1.9	1.8	1.9	1.7	1.7
Fabricated metal products, machinery and equipment	5.6	6.8	5.6	4.9	4.0	4.5	4.2	3.9
Electricity, gas and water	1.9	2.1	3.5	3.1	0.6	0.8	0.9	0.8
Construction	7.7	7.1	5.7	6.9	9.5	10.1	9.5	9.9
Services	50.6	49.5	52.5	56.4	34.4	36.8	39.9	45.2
of which: Wholesale and retail trade, restaurants, and hotels	21.4	21.7	22.4	19.8	13.0	13.4	13.6	17.2
Transport, storage and communication	5.6	5.5	7.7	5.4	4.6	4.5	4.4	4.4
Finance, insurance, real estate and business services	10.7	10.5	10.1	13.1	2.2	2.6	3.0	3.2

Source: OECD, *National Accounts.*

BASIC STATISTICS:

INTERNATIONAL COMPARISONS

	Units	Reference period [1]	Australia	Austria
Population				
Total	Thousands	1991	17 292	7 823
Inhabitants per sq. km	Number	1991	2	93
Net average annual increase over previous 10 years	%	1991	1.5	0.3
Employment				
Total civilian employment (TCE) [2]	Thousands	1991	7 705	3 482
Of which: Agriculture	% of TCE		5.5	7.4
Industry	% of TCE		24.2	36.9
Services	% of TCE		70.4	55.8
Gross domestic product (GDP)				
At current prices and current exchange rates	Bill. US$	1991	297.4	164.7
Per capita	US$		17 200	21 048
At current prices using current PPP's [3]	Bill. US$	1991	280	135.6
Per capita	US$		16 195	17 329
Average annual volume growth over previous 5 years	%	1991	2.8	3.3
Gross fixed capital formation (GFCF)	% of GDP	1991	20.5	25.1
Of which: Machinery and equipment	% of GDP		8.8	10.4
Residential construction	% of GDP		4.6	4.6 (*)
Average annual volume growth over previous 5 years	%	1991	0.3	5.2
Gross saving ratio [4]	% of GDP	1991	17.2	25.6
General government				
Current expenditure on goods and services	% of GDP	1991	18.3	18.2
Current disbursements [5]	% of GDP	1991	36.6	45.7
Current receipts	% of GDP	1991	33.7	47.2
Net official development assistance	% of GDP	1991	0.35	0.33
Indicators of living standards				
Private consumption per capita using current PPP's [3]	US$	1991	9 827	9 591
Passenger cars, per 1 000 inhabitants	Number	1990	430	382
Telephones, per 1 000 inhabitants	Number	1990	448 (89)	589
Television sets, per 1 000 inhabitants	Number	1989	484	475
Doctors, per 1 000 inhabitants	Number	1991	2	2.1
Infant mortality per 1 000 live births	Number	1991	7.1	7.4
Wages and prices (average annual increase over previous 5 years)				
Wages (earnings or rates according to availability)	%	1991	5.4	5.2
Consumer prices	%	1991	6.7	2.5
Foreign trade				
Exports of goods, fob*	Mill. US$	1991	39 764	40 985
As % of GDP	%		13.4	24.9
Average annual increase over previous 5 years	%		13.2	12.8
Imports of goods, cif*	Mill. US$	1991	38 844	48 914
As % of GDP	%		13.1	29.7
Average annual increase over previous 5 years	%		10.1	13.7
Total official reserves [6]	Mill. SDR's	1991	11 432	6 591
As ratio of average monthly imports of goods	Ratio		3.5	1.6

*   At current prices and exchange rates.
1.   Unless otherwise stated.
2.   According to the definitions used in OECD *Labour Force Statistics*.
3.   PPP's = Purchasing Power Parities.
4.   Gross saving = Gross national disposable income minus private and government consumption.
5.   Current disbursements = Current expenditure on goods and services plus current transfers and payments of property income.
6.   Gold included in reserves is valued at 35 SDR's per ounce. End of year.
7.   Including Luxembourg.